Welfare and Planning:

an Analysis of Capitalism versus Socialism

Introduction to Economics Series

Kenyon A. Knopf, *Editor*

ECONOMIC DEVELOPMENT AND GROWTH
Robert E. Baldwin

THE ECONOMICS OF POVERTY
Alan B. Batchelder

NATIONAL INCOME AND EMPLOYMENT ANALYSIS
Arnold Collery

THE MARKET SYSTEM
Robert H. Haveman and Kenyon A. Knopf

INTERNATIONAL ECONOMIC PROBLEMS
James C. Ingram

WELFARE AND PLANNING: AN ANALYSIS OF
CAPITALISM VERSUS SOCIALISM
Heinz Köhler

TOWARD ECONOMIC STABILITY
Maurice W. Lee

CASE STUDIES IN AMERICAN INDUSTRY
Leonard W. Weiss

Welfare and Planning:
an Analysis of Capitalism
versus Socialism

HEINZ KÖHLER
Amherst College

John Wiley & Sons, Inc.   New York • London • Sydney

To my wife, Mary Elaine

Introduction to Economics Series

Teachers of introductory economics seem to agree on the impracticality of presenting a comprehensive survey of economics to freshmen or sophomores. Many of them believe there is a need for some alternative which provides a solid core of principles while permitting an instructor to introduce a select set of problems and applied ideas. This series attempts to fill that need and also to give the interested layman a set of self-contained books that he can absorb with interest and profit, without assistance.

By offering greater flexibility in the choice of topics for study, these books represent a more realistic and reasonable approach to teaching economics than most of the large, catchall textbooks. With separate volumes and different authors for each topic, the instructor is not as tied to a single track as in the omnibus introductory economics text.

Underlying the series is the pedagogical premise that students should be introduced to economics by learning how economists think about economic problems. Thus the concepts and relationships of elementary economics are presented to the student in conjunction with a few economic problems. An approach of this kind offers a good beginning to the student who intends to move on to advanced work and furnishes a clearer understanding for those whose study of economics is limited to an introductory exposure. Teachers and students alike should find the books helpful and stimulating.

Kenyon A. Knopf, Editor

Preface

The issue of Socialism versus Capitalism is likely to draw a highly emotional response in most places. A man in New York may very well insist that socialism is bad, although he probably does not know anything about it, while his counterpart in Peking may be in the same position with respect to capitalism. Many followers of Marx refuse to question his authority. They *know* that capitalism is bound to collapse on its own and that socialism alone can genuinely concern itself for the welfare of mankind, and there is no room for discussion with the unbeliever. The followers of the American way of life are not less bigoted. Our beliefs are also a citadel to be defended, not a hypothesis to be discussed.

All too often we refuse to accept the fact that reasonable people may hold beliefs that other reasonable people may regard as fantastic. Actually it might not hurt to expose ourselves to new points of view, to self-examine rather than to self-justify, to engage in dialogue rather than to preach. If there is to be hope for the survival of mankind, we must cease to see our way of life as the only natural one.

Just as man had to learn that this planet is not the center of the universe, we must become conscious of our misplaced tendencies, as societies and as persons, to regard ourselves as the center of righteousness. We must agree to differ or we may cease to exist in an explosion of violence. We have to learn to talk with each other, to respect each other, rather than try to destroy each other. This book, it is hoped, will contribute to this discussion.

It is not assumed that the reader has any previous knowledge of economics. Any intelligent person willing to make the effort should be able to follow the main theme, which is to present, as simply and lucidly as possible, the issues involved in considering alternative economic systems. In this book, welfare economics is developed at an introductory but rigorous level, and tools of modern economic analysis, such as input-output analysis and linear programming, are introduced as needed.

The stress throughout the first eight chapters is on theory, on the presentation of models of economic systems. It is my belief that only such simplified abstractions from reality can provide the map to guide us through the chaos of reality. These models are essential tools for any proper analysis of actual living economies because they put into sharp relief alternative answers to the fundamental question of economic organization. This book, being lean and concise, may appear to be easy. The student might do well, however, to examine these chapters again and again, for once he has really mastered what is being done here, he will have a firm hold on the essence of the fundamental ideas of economic organization. Only then will he be really ready for a look at reality.

A look at reality is provided in Chapters 9 to 11, with emphasis on the Soviet economy. Any other one would have served equally well to illustrate that any economy in the world is an imperfect copy of any model discussed in this book or of a combination of several of them. The Soviet economy was chosen because most readers are likely to be familiar, from personal experience or prior study of economics, with the broad features of a capitalist economy. In this latter part of the book, conciseness has again been my deliberate goal. Other books of a descriptive and institutional nature are never hard to find. My own *Economic Integration in the Soviet Bloc** is a case in point. Furthermore, eastern European institutional structures are in a state of flux. It seemed to me beside the point to discuss them in more detail than has been provided here. The point of this book is to communicate fundamental theoretical concepts and to get them across so well that any reader can study any descriptive material on any economy in the world and read tomorrow about tomorrow's institutional changes and still understand "what is going on."

Apart from use by the intelligent layman, a number of scholarly uses of this book suggest themselves. There will be those teaching elementary economics at a rigorous level who might welcome

---

* Praeger, New York, 1965.

such a volume as a follow-up to the traditional study of the market economy. To be realistic, this would require more than the typical one week on socialism found in many introductory courses, and it would also require a great deal of support of the student by his instructor. Those willing and able to devote to it the necessary time are likely, however, to find this study an exciting experience. I have found it so, with students of mine. It might make for an unorthodox introductory course, but it might also give students the excitement and lasting understanding that economics, properly taught, can bring about.

On the other hand, there will be those who will find this volume eminently useful in teaching economic theory at the intermediate level. Juniors and seniors, as we all know, are not beyond improvement in their understanding of the basic problems of resource allocation, and they will welcome a study which shows how a variety of economic tools with which they have become acquainted can be used and fit together.

Finally, the students and teachers of comparative-systems courses may find here a welcome change from the emphasis on description and from stress on information that quickly depreciates. As a novel approach to many comparative-systems courses, this text may provide a less ephemeral theoretical core around which any desired institutional material may be built and examined.

I must mention gratefully a former teacher of mine, Kenneth E. Boulding, of the University of Michigan. His teaching and writing (see Bibliography), more than anyone else's, have caused me to work on this book. His superb ability to use the English language in the teaching of economics (and so much more) has helped immeasurably my own understanding and teaching. In fact, many of his formulations were so happily chosen that they have remained with me for many years, and every once in a while I have discovered that one of my particularly well-chosen phrases or examples was his and not mine at all. I owe him a great debt.

I thank my colleague Arnold Collery, who has read the manuscript and made a number of suggestions for improvement. Also I express my sincere gratitude to Mrs. Mildred Buzicky for creating, as usual, a beautiful typescript in record-breaking time. Finally, I am greatly indebted to many fellow economists and, particularly, fellow specialists on the economies of eastern Europe, whose writings have been an inspiration to me. Since this is intended as a textbook, however, I have tried to hold footnote references to a minimum. A bibliography of the most important works used in my preparation of the manuscript is found at the back of this volume and will serve both as an acknowledgment to my colleagues and as an inducement to the interested reader for further reading adventures.

HEINZ KÖHLER

Contents

Chapter 1   **Introduction**   **1**

     I.   Scarcity the Basic Problem   2
     II.   The Productive Process   3
     III.   Capitalism and Socialism   4

Chapter 2   **The Goals of Full Employment and Efficiency**   **6**

     I.   Full Use of Resources   6
     II.   Efficient Use of Resources   7
           A. The Conditions   7
           B. Summary   25

Chapter 3   **The Goals of Equity and Growth**   **27**

     I.   Equitable Distribution of Output   27
     II.   Sufficient Growth of Output   33

Chapter 4   **Perfectly Competitive Capitalism**   **36**

     I.   The Conditions   36
     II.   The Markets   38
     III.   The Price System   44
     IV.   The Level of Employment   45
     V.   The Degree of Efficiency   47
     VI.   The Rational Price System Defined   52
     VII.   The Distribution of Income   53
     VIII. The Growth of Output   53

Chapter 5   **Capitalist Reality and Socialist Critique**   **54**

     I.   The Likelihood of Unemployment   54
     II.   The Problem of Inefficiency   55

III. Inequities in Income Distribution 56
IV. Insufficient Growth 57
V. Enter the Socialists 58
    A. Increasing Returns 58
    B. Need for Collective Consumption 61
    C. Externalities 62
    D. Summary 66

Chapter 6 Socialism: The Competitive Solution 67

I. A Famous Debate 68
II. The Model 69
III. An Illustration 72
IV. The Claims 76
V. The Criticism 78

Chapter 7 Socialism: The Centralist Scheme I 82

I. The Use of Input-Output Analysis 83
    A. The Transactions Table 83
    B. Direct Technical Coefficients 88
    C. Planning by Iteration 90
    D. Practical Problems and the Use of Computers 94
    E. Criticism of the Model 102

Chapter 8 Socialism: The Centralist Scheme II 106

I. The Use of Linear Programming 106
    A. Single Production Technique 107
    B. Several Production Techniques 115
    C. Shadow Prices 121

Chapter 9 The Soviet Economy 123

I. Goals and Strategy 123
II. The Planning Mechanism 126
III. The Role of Prices and Money 129
    A. A Digression: Marxian Ideology 130
    B. Industrial Wholesale Prices 132
    C. Agricultural Prices 133
    D. Retail Prices and the Labor Market 133
    E. State Bank Control 136

F. Incentives and Their Effects   136

IV.   Soviet Economic Performance Evaluated   141

Chapter 10   The Great Debate   144

I.   Weaknesses Examined   144
  A. Antiquated Planning Methods and Incentives   144
  B. Economic Inefficiency   147

II.   Remedies Suggested   150
  A. Central Mathematical Planning   150
  B. Decentralization and the Use of Market Forces   154
  C. The Need for Price Reform   155

III.   Experiments outside the USSR   156
IV.   Summary   158

Chapter 11   An All-Important Question   160

I.   What of Freedom and Human Dignity   162

Bibliography   165

Index   169

1

Introduction

Human wants are infinite in size and variety. Let us imagine a genie, appearing to a man and holding before him the possibility of gaining everything he desired. Even in a few minutes a man could compile an impressive list of things, seen and unseen, which he would want to have or do or be, if only he could. There would parade before his mind the many kinds of food, clothing, houses, cars, the image of doctors who help, of friends who care, of a wife who loves. He would be thinking of concerts to attend, of playing in the sun, of a satisfying job, of liberty, courage, wisdom, and the ability to love. Given enough time, the list might be endless or, perhaps, he might cross out all but one wish! Surely, though, as we imagine our genie asking everyone in the human family, the ingredients of welfare so compiled will defy anyone's ability to measure and count.

Suppose, however, that we wished to arrange life on earth so as to fulfill human wants as much as possible. Clearly, this would be a colossal task and require the imagination and energy of all of mankind. There would be room for everyone: for the peace-makers whose efforts reconcile conflicting wants as well as for the producers whose toil can satisfy basic needs. Thus we are led directly to an important distinction. It is impossible to *measure* the quantities of peace and justice and love "produced" by friends or poets or diplomats, though hardly possible to deny their importance for human welfare. On the other hand, it is quite possible to measure the production of loaves of bread, and houses, and suits of clothing. In fact, it is exactly this latter world of measurable quantities of things produced, exchanged, and consumed which has become the subject matter of economic analysis. *Pure economics* tries to explain the relationships among such measurable quantities and among ratios derived from them, abstracting completely from the human actors behind the stage. Another branch of economics, however, goes beyond these seemingly mechanical relationships and deals specifically with the question how this world of measurable, producible goods, and any change therein, affects human welfare. It is aptly called *welfare economics* and will be central to much of our discussion in the next chapters.

I. SCARCITY, THE BASIC PROBLEM

To begin, it is well to hold before us the central concern of the economist with the problem of *scarcity*. This refers to the scarcity of producible goods in relation to human wants for them. These scarce goods can be material (commodities such as bread or schools or battleships) or nonmaterial (services such as those of doctors or teachers or barbers), but they all have in common that they can be produced in measurable quantities. Since total human welfare depends on much more than such outputs of the economy, the economist is clearly dealing with only part of that welfare. We shall refer to this component as *economic* welfare. Given all other factors affecting it, total welfare can be increased by increasing economic welfare. This involves reducing the scarcity of goods as far as possible.

Hence the economist is inevitably led to question why goods are scarce or what could make them more abundant. The answer is, of course, that goods are scarce because the ingredients needed for their production are available only in limited amounts and our knowledge of how to use them, of the recipe of production as it were, is far from perfect. Therefore, overcoming scarcity involves using those ingredients as sparingly as possible in order to get the most out of them. Indeed, it is from the necessity of *economizing* scarce productive resources that economics gets its name.

II. THE PRODUCTIVE PROCESS

Traditionally such resources are called factors of production or inputs, and they are categorized into three major groupings. First, there is *labor,* including any and all types of *human effort* put forth in the process of production. The quantity of labor which a society has depends on the size of the population, even more on the proportion of the population working and on the time each person works per day. In addition, the productiveness of labor will vary with the quantity and kind of food and medical care available, with the degree of education and cultural enrichment, and in general with the value society puts on working hard. Second, there is the group of inputs referred to as *land.* This includes all the nonhuman *gifts of nature* entering the productive process. Part of this category is, of course, agricultural land itself, so widely varying in usefulness, depending on the topography, temperature, humidity and fertility of the area. Other natural resources, such as mineral resources and water power, also form part of this grouping. Depending on the ease of extraction, refining, and transportation, the quantity and quality of minerals available will also vary greatly over time and space. Finally, there is *capital,* the sum total of all *man-made productive inputs.* This includes buildings, all types of machinery and equipment, and inventories of materials including semifinished and finished goods.

We must realize, however, that what these inputs can produce depends to a large extent on the *environment* in which they are put to use. *Technology,* the types of knowledge available and used in the productive process, is of enormous importance in the determination of output from given inputs. Until one discovers how to improve plants and animals through selective breeding, or to eliminate impurities from ores, or to produce vast amounts of electric or nuclear power, any given set of inputs will be much less productive of outputs than after such discovery and application of knowledge. Indeed, prior to such knowledge, available inputs may not even be recognized as such and may be regarded as completely useless. Similarly, the extent to which production is organized on the basis of *specialization and exchange,* rather than self-sufficiency of any person or region, will help to influence powerfully the output producible from given inputs. Finally, the general system of *economic control,* the type of institutional framework within which economic activity is carried out, including who makes decisions on the basis of what kind of incentives, will serve to determine the productivity of the productive factors.

III. CAPITALISM AND SOCIALISM

An example of the latter is organization of production through a capitalist or socialist order. We have already in our hands the concepts needed to illustrate the basic difference between these two types of economic control. *A capitalist economic system is one in which land and capital,* that is, all nonhuman factors of production, *are privately owned and utilized.* On the other hand, *under socialism these very inputs are collectively owned* by a group of people (often all citizens of a nation) *and collectively put to use,* usually through the government acting as a trustee of the people. Given this simple definition, it is immediately clear that the basic economic problem, scarcity, must be the same in capitalism and socialism. If scarcity of goods is partly due to the limited availability of inputs, the introduction of socialism will hardly of itself alleviate scarcity. Inputs do not suddenly become less scarce by being publicly owned rather than privately owned. It is also hard to believe that the introduction of socialism suddenly changes human nature, reducing wants to the available means for satisfying them, thereby eliminating scarcity. However, there remains the question whether socialism *over time* will be better able to *increase* the quantities of inputs than capitalism or whether the change in the environment itself in which given resources are used will be such as to improve their productivity under socialism. These are questions to which we shall turn later in the course of this book.

Leaving aside for the moment the issue whether the socialist system of economic control can overcome scarcity *more than* the capitalist, there is no doubt that it also is not able to overcome scarcity fully. Hence the socialist as well as the capitalist economist faces scarcity as his basic challenge. It is no wonder then that the major areas of concern of economists in capitalism and in socialism are also the same. Both are highly interested in the full and efficient use of resources, in an equitable distribution of output, and in sufficient growth of output over time. That is not to say, of course, that both—the adherents of the capitalist and socialist orders—consider each of these four goals to be *equally* important. But they both consider them to be *the* important goals of the economic system. We now turn, therefore, to a discussion of these goals, thereby setting the stage for the major purpose of this book, an examination of socialist blueprints and reality as contrasted with capitalism.

2

The Goals of Full Employment and Efficiency

I. FULL USE OF RESOURCES

It is not difficult to see why economists everywhere advocate the *full employment of resources.* If the basic problem is scarcity, that is, if, even by using resources fully, no single society is able to produce enough to satisfy everyone's economic wants, and if we want to maximize economic welfare, then it would be utter folly to leave some resources unemployed. By so doing, we would forego some possible production and hence not fulfill our calling. Although everyone will agree with this, full employment is by no means a clear-cut concept. Even in the short run, the amount of labor used, for example, could be varied significantly by changes in the working age, the hours worked per day, as well as the days worked per year. There is nothing to prevent us from trying to use our capital stock 24 hours per day, and we *could* strive to use every acre of land for agricultural purposes, or to mine our mineral resources at the fastest rate circumstances allow. Clearly, here is room for quarrel even among reasonable men. As wartime conditions show, the full employment ceiling is certainly a flexible one, and it can be raised by a variety of means, such as appeal to patriotism or brute force. The latter suggests that it is quite possible to "trade" one kind of welfare for another, a subject to which we shall return. By restricting a person's freedom to decide whether, where, for how long, and in which occupation he wants to work, for example, the output of goods may well be increased. But in this case noneconomic welfare has been sacrificed for economic welfare, possibly contrary to the wishes of the person concerned. To avoid this undesirable side effect, many economists define full employment as the state of affairs wherein all resources are used at the rate at which their owners want to have them used. To sum up, economists everywhere agree that full use of resources is desirable, but there is no agreement on how full is full.

II. EFFICIENT USE OF RESOURCES

There is, however, general agreement on the meaning of *efficient employment of resources*. What is meant by it must be spelled out in great detail. Although all resources are fully employed, by whatever definition of that term, they might at the same time be used inefficiently, yielding a smaller satisfaction of economic wants than would be possible after some reorganization in the economy. In a general way, efficiency can be defined as the state of affairs where all *unambiguous* possibilities for increasing economic welfare have been exhausted. Put in another way it is *a state of the economy wherein it is impossible to make anyone better off without making someone else worse off*. Obviously, if it were possible to do such a thing, total economic welfare could be increased with certainty and, if efficiency is our goal, it should be done. On the other hand, if it is only possible to increase one person's economic welfare *at the expense* of another's, we cannot be certain how total economic welfare has changed, if it has changed at all, unless we are prepared to compare the absolute amounts of satisfaction of different persons. This involves conflict, questions of equity, and it is a task we shall discuss in the following chapter. In the meantime we shall concentrate on achieving efficiency alone, on making use of all unambiguous possibilities for increasing total economic welfare.

A. The Conditions

These possibilities are often presented as the "seven marginal conditions." They are also referred to as the conditions of the "Pareto optimum," Vilfredo Pareto being one of the first economists who spelled out in detail the implications of the goal of economic efficiency as defined here[1]: fulfilling any marginal condition assures that it is impossible to make anyone better off without making someone else worse off.

The *first marginal condition* deals with the *optimum allocation of goods at a given time,* the goods being assumed to have already been produced and distributed. It states:

> The marginal rate of substitution (MRS) between any two goods, *a* and *b*, must be the same for any two consumers, *A* and *B*, having both goods.

$$MRS^A_{a,b} = MRS^B_{a,b}$$

Table 2-1

	Initial Situation		Type of Change	Final Situation	
	Quantities Possessed	MRS		Quantities Possessed	MRS
Consumer A	10a and 30b	1a = 2b	Exchange of goods	9a and 32b	1a = 2.7b
Consumer B	7a and 15b	1a = 3b		8a and 13b	1a = 2.7b
	17a and 45b			17a and 45b	

This can be most easily illustrated with the numerical example in Table 2-1. Suppose *A* to possess originally 10 units of *a* and 30 of *b*, while *B* possesses less of both, say, 7*a* and 15*b*. Now we would argue that every person is able to make a *subjective* evaluation of the relative worth to him of goods such as *a* and *b*. Consumer *A* in our example initially values 1*a* as much as 2*b*. This exchange ratio *in his mind* is called the marginal rate of substitution or MRS. It is clearly a purely subjective magnitude, telling us that Consumer *A* would give up 1*a* for 2*b* or 2*b* for 1*a* and feel neither worse nor better off. He is indifferent about exchange at that rate *under the given circumstances,* which are

---

[1] *Cours d'Economie Politique* (Lausanne, 1897), Vol. II, pp. 364 ff., and *Manuel d'Economie Politique* (Paris, 1910), pp. 362 ff.

defined by his possessing 10*a* and 30*b* and unknown quantities of other goods *c*, *d*, *e*, etc. This is the reason for talking about a *marginal* rate of substitution or exchange. Under the given circumstances, our consumer is willing to make a slight (marginal) adjustment in his possessions. But though he is willing to exchange 1*a* for 2*b*, since he would feel equally well off according to his own estimate, can we assume that he would also be willing to give up 10*a* for 20*b*? Introspection alone will suggest that this will probably *not* be the case. More likely than not, as the quantity of anything in our possession increases, given all other quantities, our total economic welfare or utility will rise, yet the *extra* welfare or *marginal* utility brought by each additional unit of the good will decrease. However much we enjoyed our first car, the *extra* enjoyment (marginal utility) derived from the second or third or fourth is likely to be successively less, even though our *total* well-being may continue to rise. Hence it is this *principle of diminishing marginal utility* which tells us that consumer *A*, were he to leave his original situation and exchange 1*a* for 2*b*, would *thereafter* view the situation differently. Having more *b*, he would probably value each *b* less than before, even if he had the same of *a*, more so if he had less of it. Having less *a*, he might value each *a* more. If he were asked again to give up 1*a*, he might demand more than 2*b* for it, precisely because *to him* the value of *a* has risen, of *b* fallen. We shall expect, therefore, that any actual exchange will alter the MRS according to the principle of diminishing (or rising) marginal utility with greater (or smaller) quantities possessed.

Just as the MRS will be different for a *given* individual, depending on the circumstances, it will differ *among* individuals. In our example, consumer *B* is assumed to own originally 7*a* and 15*b* and be willing to exchange indifferently 1*a* for 3*b* or 3*b* for 1*a*. This *may* be due to the fact that he finds himself in different circumstances, having different quantities of all goods from *A*. But his MRS would probably differ even if he had the same quantities of *a*, *b*, and all other goods. This is likely to be true because tastes, as we all know, differ among people, and *B* might under *any and all* circumstances value *a* more highly than *b*. In any case, in our example, he initially does, and this implies that the first marginal condition is *not* fulfilled. Hence we can increase welfare by allocating goods more efficiently so that *those for whom a good is relatively more useful get more of it.* A hypothetical exchange of goods between A and B, shown above, illustrates the point. A, by giving up 1a and getting 2b, ends up with 9a and 32b, leaving him by his own judgment (original MRS: 1a = 2b) equally well off. B, by giving up 2b and getting 1a, ends up with 8a and 13b, and he is *better off.* By his own estimate, he would have been equally well off had he given up 3b (original MRS: 1a = 3b). He had to give up less than that. The exchange of goods has increased the welfare of one person without reducing that of anyone else.

Note that the actual exchange could have occurred at any rate from 1a = 2b to 1a = 3b, limits which are suggested by the original two MRS. Had the exchange occurred at the rate of 1a = 3b, only A would have gained, but B would not have lost. At any intermediate rate of exchange, both consumers would have shared in the welfare gain through increased efficiency.

As long as any divergence in marginal rates of substitution persists such gains are possible. In our example, it has been conveniently assumed that after the first round of exchange, both consumers adjust their subjective evaluations so that both now value 1a as much as 2.7b. To A, good a is now subjectively worth more, good b worth less, as he has more of the latter, but less of the former. For B the exact opposite holds. Given our example, the first marginal condition is now fulfilled, and further exchange could not improve allocative efficiency, yielding an increase in economic welfare.

It should also be noted that the example could be extended to any number of consumers and products. For *any* combination of consumers, Z and Q, F and G, A and C, etc., as well as for *any* combination of goods, e and f, r and s, x and n, the condition must be fulfilled for maximum efficiency.

The position of the economy at the moment of fulfillment is, however, by no means unique. In our example, a final situation in which A owned 1a and 2b and B owned 16a and 43b would have been just as efficient as long as the final MRS had been the same for both. This illustrates that we are now only determining what *kind* of goods should go to whom, not *how much* output *in general* a person should get.

Those well versed in elementary economic theory will have noted that the first marginal condition is in fact demanding that any two consumers should be consuming a combination of any two goods such that their marginal utility ratios are equal. If the MRS for A is $1a = 2b$, he is in fact saying that his ratio of marginal utility of b to marginal utility of a equals $\frac{1}{2}$.

$$MRS^A_{a,b} = \left(\frac{MU_b}{MU_a}\right)_A = \frac{1}{2}$$

Only if the extra satisfaction (marginal utility) gained from each b is half that of each a, will A indifferently substitute $2b$ for $1a$. (The rate of indifferent substitution is graphically expressed by the slope of an indifference curve.) Fulfilling the first condition, therefore, assures that

$$\left(\frac{MU_a}{MU_b}\right)_A = \left(\frac{MU_a}{MU_b}\right)_B$$

The *second marginal condition* concerns the *optimum degree of specialization in production:*

> The marginal rate of transformation (MRT) between any two goods, a and b, must be the same for any two firms, α and β, producing both goods.

$$MRT^\alpha_{a,b} = MRT^\beta_{a,b}$$

This will again be illustrated (Table 2-2) with a numerical example.

Table 2-2.

	Initial Situation		Type of Change	Final Situation	
	Output per Period	MRT		Output per Period	MRT
Producer α	15a and 50b	$1a = 2b$	Reallocation of	16a and 48b	$1a = 2.5b$
Producer β	15a and 10b	$1a = 3b$	production by	14a and 13b	$1a = 2.5b$
	30a and 60b		shifting inputs within producing units	30a and 61b	

We now suppose that producers α and β originally produce products a and b at the rate indicated in the table, totalling 30a and 60b per period. Every producer is able to determine the *objective technical* rate at which goods a and b can be substituted. This can be done for example by, *not* producing 1a and using the resources so released to produce as much b as is technically possible. For α this rate of exchange, called the marginal rate of transformation or MRT, is $1a = 2b$, for β it is $1a = 3b$. In short, while α can produce 1a or 2b with identical inputs, β can produce 1a or 3b with identical inputs, inputs which might well differ from the set of inputs involved in α! In the case of α, it "costs" as much labor, land, and capital *under the given circumstances* to produce 1a as it would to produce 2b. This is once more the reason for calling this a *marginal* rate of transformation between products. This type of small (marginal) adjustment is possible under given circumstances. Though α, given its present state of resource use for the production of 15a and 50b and unknown amounts of other products, could "transform" 1a into 2b by refraining to produce the former and using the resources so saved to make 2b, can it also cut production of a by 10, increasing that of b by 20? This might or might not be possible. We can easily conceive of a situation in which we wish to increase output of b at the expense of output of a. At first we shall cut output of a by taking the resources best at making b, but the farther we proceed along this path, the less suited as to quality or proportions for b might be the resources used in a, and the less might b output rise for given sacrifices of a. Alternatively, the greater might sacrifices in a have to be to achieve equal increases in the output of b. This is the *principle of increasing marginal cost* which tells us that α, were it to leave its original position and produce one less a to make 2 more b, might *thereafter* not be able to do it again at the same MRT. As we shift labor from farms to industry, for example, a given increase in industrial output might at first involve only a negligible decline in agricultural product, as we shift those people and types of equipment least suited to agriculture and most apt for industrial work. But eventually the same rise in industrial output might be arranged only at much greater cost in agricultural products foregone (it is called *opportunity cost*), as the best farm labor and equipment leave farms to be ineptly used in the factories. It is quite *possible*, therefore, that increases or decreases in output of any product will go hand in hand with increases or decreases in the marginal cost of producing that product (in the sense of opportunity foregone to produce something else).

Just as the MRT will differ for a *given* firm depending on circumstances, so will it differ *among* firms. In our example, firm β is assumed to produce initially 15*a* and 10*b* and, unlike α, is able to transform technically 1*a* into 3*b* or vice versa. This *may* be due to the difference in production levels, but again the two MRT might differ if both producers produced identical quantities of all goods, if, for instance, they possessed different technical know-how or different types of inputs.

In any case, in our example the initial MRT do differ; hence the second marginal condition is not fulfilled. We can increase economic welfare by allocating production more efficiently so that *the producer who is relatively better (relatively low cost) at making a good produces more of it.* In our case, α is that firm for good *a*, which in terms of *b* foregone is cheaper there than for β. Firm α should produce more of, that is, specialize in *a*, while β should specialize in *b*. As the table indicates, α could by producing 2 less *b* free enough resources to produce one more *a*. If β at the same time were to produce one less *a*, it would have sufficient resources to make 3 more *b*. Clearly, aggregate output then is increased by 1*b*. If there was full employment before, there is now, for the same amounts of resources are used. They have only been shifted *within* α from activity *b* to activity *a*, *within* β from activity *a* to activity *b*. Efficiency has clearly increased. No matter who gets the extra output, it is *possible* to make someone better off without making anyone worse off. This could be done in a variety of ways, as also by leaving the output of *a* and *b* unchanged and using the resources capable of producing 1*b* in β to produce *c* instead.

As long as any divergence in the MRT persists, the gain from specialization can be further increased. In our example, it has been assumed that after the first adjustment, because of increasing marginal costs, the new MRT are equal at 1*a* = 2.5*b*. For α the sacrifice of *b* involved in increasing output of *a* *again* has risen. The same would be true if β tried to raise *b* output by an equal amount once more. It would now have to sacrifice not $1a$ but $1.2a$ for $3b$. Further specialization would bring no further gain. By the same reasoning it could be shown that only *complete* specialization assures maximum efficiency in the case of constant, rather than rising, marginal costs. If in our example the original MRT never changed, α should produce not only more, but *nothing but a, β nothing but b.*

Those who have had an introduction to economics will possibly recognize that the second marginal condition is nothing else but the famous law of comparative advantage. Producers α and β can be thought of not only as two firms within a country, but also as regions or countries themselves. Everything that has been said would then apply equally. As with the first marginal condition, this one, too, should hold for *any* combination of producers, however defined, and any combination of products, if maximum efficiency is to pertain. Also as with the first condition, one can conceive of an infinite variety of situations which would be efficient. There is no unique solution. The condition would be fulfilled even if in the end α produced $1a$ and $1b$, and β $39a$ and $500b$, *as long as* their MRT were equal at whatever level. Analogous statements hold true for the other marginal conditions to be discussed, though this will not be repeated each time. Those knowledgeable in theory might also have noted that the second marginal condition demands that any two producers should be producing a combination of any two goods such that their marginal cost ratios are equal. If the MRT for α is $1a = 2b$, it is in fact stating that its ratio of marginal cost of b to marginal cost of a equals $\frac{1}{2}$.

$$MRT^{\alpha}_{a,b} = \left(\frac{MC_b}{MC_a} \right)_{\alpha} = \frac{1}{2}$$

Only if the extra resource (Marginal Cost) of each b is half that of each a, will α be able to transform $2b$ into $1a$ or vice versa. (This rate of technical transformation is graphically expressed by the slope of the production possibility curve.) Fulfilling the second condition, therefore, assures that

$$\left(\frac{MC_a}{MC_b} \right)_a = \left(\frac{MC_a}{MC_b} \right)_\beta$$

The *third marginal condition* deals with the *optimum resource allocation among producers.*

The marginal rate of transformation (MRT) between any resource x and any product a must be the same for any two producers, α and β, producing this product with that resource.

$$MRT^\alpha_{x,a} = MRT^\beta_{x,a}$$

Table 2-3 shows our convenient numerical example.

Table 2-3.

	Initial Situation			Final Situation	
	Input and Output per Period	MRT	Type of Change	Input and Output per Period	MRT
Producer α	20x make 40a	1x = 2a	Moving of in-	19x make 38a	1x = 2.2a
Producer β	20x make 60a	1x = 3a	put from one	21x make 63a	1x = 2.2a
	40x make 100a		producer to another	40x make 101a	

Suppose there are two producers producing an identical product a with at least one identical input x. Each producer can determine the *objective technical* rate at which x is used up to make a. Under given circumstances, including which other inputs are used, which outputs are produced, etc., α could produce 2 more a, if it had 1 more unit of resource x. Again, however, we are warned by the term *marginal* rate of transformation, that the above is a technical possibility for a marginal adjustment.[2] It might *not* be possible for α to produce 200 extra a, if it had only 100 more x. Probably a, like most goods, is produced by more than one input. If we *only* increased the input of x, but not of y, z, etc., output might well increase, but by less and less for equal doses of x as we proceed. Inputs y, z, etc., sooner or later are bound to become overworked. We are meeting here the

[2] It is a numerical accident that in our example the average rates of transformation are equal to the marginal rates in the initial situation. The ART for α is $40a/20x = 2a/1x$, and for β it is $60a/20x = 3a/1x$.

famous *principle of diminishing marginal returns*. As we keep adding equal doses of fertilizer (x) to a fixed amount of land, labor, seed, and equipment (y, z, etc.), corn output (a) may well rise for a while, but it is certain to rise by less and less (diminishing marginal physical product) and eventually will even fall absolutely. If this were not so, we could grow the world's annual crop of corn on a single acre or even in a single flowerpot!

Therefore, the MRT will differ for a *given* firm depending on circumstances. So will it differ among firms, either because, as with α and β above, they might through different know-how, produce different quantities of output with identical inputs, or because they are likely to be using different quantities and types of inputs. (In the case above, although β is using as much x as α, β might use more or better y, z, etc.)

Again in our case the third marginal condition is not fulfilled to begin with. Economic welfare can be increased by shifting x from α to β, that is, toward the high productivity firm. In our example, although output produced by α drops by $2a$, as $1x$ is transferred from α to β, output of β rises by $3a$. *The producer who is absolutely better at using an input should get more of it.* Aggregate output is up and everyone *could* fare as well as before the reorganization, or better.

As long as the divergence in the MRT exists, such gain can be had. In our example, it was again assumed that, after the first adjustment, the MRT have converged, excluding further improvement. Producer β, having more x but no more of other inputs, has experienced diminishing returns. Were he to add another x *now*, it could increase a by 2.2 only, not by 3. Producer α went backward on the road of diminishing returns, his other inputs are now relatively more abundant and, *at the margin*, x is now somewhat more productive.

As in an earlier case, there is no reason why "producer" cannot be understood as a region or even a country. "Firm" β might be California (or the entire United States), α being Alabama (or China). Input x (labor) in California (or the United States) might be so much more productive at the margin because of superior technology, capital, and land. Hence a shift of labor from Alabama to California (or from China to the United States) might increase world output, as the decrease in Alabama or China is smaller than the increase in California or the United States. Obstacles to resource mobility—whether insufficient roads, language barriers, or immigration laws—clearly constitute a barrier to the achievement of economic efficiency.

Finally, we should again note for the initiated that the third marginal condition demands in effect that the slope of the production function, relating physical quantities of any input to those of any output (other inputs being invariant), be the same at the point of production for all relevant producers.

If for α $1x$ can be made into $2a$, its $MRT_{x,a} = 1/2$. But this is the reciprocal of the extra output producible with an extra unit of input, or the marginal physical product of x in making a. $MPP_x{}^a = 2$. Therefore, the third condition assures that the marginal physical product of any input in making any output is the same for all producers.

$$\left(MPP_x{}^a \right)_\alpha = \left(MPP_x{}^a \right)_\beta$$

The *fourth marginal condition* is to achieve *optimum input combinations* for a product:

> The marginal rate of substitution of any two inputs, x and y, used in the production of any product a, must be the same for any two firms, α and β, using these two inputs to produce that product.

$$MRS^\alpha_{x,y \text{ in } a} = MRS^\beta_{x,y \text{ in } a}$$

We again present a numerical example (Table 2-4). We have two producers producing fixed and possibly different quantities of an identical product a. They both are using inputs x and y and possibly others. The amounts of x and y used originally are 30 and 35, respectively, in the aggregate. Each producer can determine the *objective technical* rate at which he can substitute inputs x and y, while leaving the quantity of output unchanged. Under given circumstances, α can keep its output unchanged by reducing input x by 1 as long as it increases input y by 2 units or vice versa. Again, however, this is a *marginal* rate of technical substitution. It holds for a slight adjustment in the original situations, but it does not assure us

Table 2-4.

	Initial Situation			Final Situation	
	Inputs Used to Produce Given Output per Period	MRS	Type of Change	Inputs Used to Produce Given Output per Period	MRS
Producer α	27x and 15y	1x = 2y	Exchanging inputs between producers	26x and 17y	1x = 2.3y
Producer β	3x and 20y	1x = 3y		4x and 17y	1x = 2.3y
	30x and 35y			30x and 34y 1y free	

that 27x could also be substituted for 54y. We have already met the *principle of diminishing marginal returns.* Although for a while increased human care might make up for less fertilizer and land in the production of corn, it would be foolish to assume that such substitution could be continued indefinitely or at a constant rate. More and more effort will be needed to keep output from falling as fertilizer and land are reduced in equal successive doses. Eventually there will be no further possibility for substitution at all.

Naturally the MRS will differ with the circumstances of the individual producer. For the same reasons discussed above in connection with the third condition, the MRS can differ among firms, as in our case they do.

Let us suppose that we arranged for an exchange of inputs between the producers (rather than a one-way shift as in condition 3). And *producers should use more of the inputs which with them are relatively more productive.* In α, at the margin, each y produces as much as $\frac{1}{2}x$, in β only as much as $\frac{1}{3}x$. Firm α should use more y. Without changing its output, it could, for instance, give up 1x for 2 y. Two more y make up exactly the potential output loss by using 1 less x. Firm β, on the other hand, can afford to release from use 3y as it receives 1x and will keep its output at its original level. Since, however, it only had to give 2y to α in exchange for 1x, 1y is released from employment altogether. Output of a has changed neither in α nor in β. The additional 1y could clearly be used somewhere in some firm to produce some good. It might, for instance, be used in β to *increase* output of a. Then economic welfare has been increased.

II. Efficient Use of Resources 19

As long as the divergence of the MRS persists, such increase in efficiency is possible. In our example, it was assumed that the final MRS have been equalized. From the law of diminishing marginal returns, we would expect each y to be less productive of output as there is more of it, even given the amount of x. In α, x has declined, making this all the more likely. While before y was as productive at the margin as 0.5 x, it is now only as productive as 0.43 x. Similarly, in β, increases in x, given y, would run into diminishing returns. This is reinforced by a cut in y. Previously each x produced as much as $3y$ at the margin, but now only as much as $2.3y$.

Finally, let us note that the fourth marginal condition demands, in effect, that any two producers should be producing a given good so that their marginal physical product ratios are equal. If the MRS for α is $lx = 2y$, it is saying that its ratio of marginal physical product of y to marginal physical product of x in the making of a equals $\frac{1}{2}$.

$$MRS^a_{x,y \text{ in } a} = \left(\frac{MPP_y^a}{MPP_x^a}\right)_\alpha = \frac{1}{2}$$

Only if the extra product gained from one y is half that of one x, can α substitute $2y$ for lx and keep output the same. (The rate of technical substitution is graphically expressed by the slope of an iso-product curve). Fulfilling the fourth condition, therefore, assures that

$$\left(\frac{MPP_x^a}{MPP_y^a}\right)_\alpha = \left(\frac{MPP_x^a}{MPP_y^a}\right)_\beta$$

The *fifth marginal condition* is concerned with the *optimum direction of production:*

> The marginal rate of substitution between any two products, a and b, for any consumer, A, must equal the marginal rate of transformation between these two products for any producer, α, producing both.

$$MRS^A_{a,b} = MRT^\alpha_{a,b}$$

At random, from among millions of consumers and thousands of firms, we select A and α who have in common that they

Table 2-5.

	Initial Situation			Final Situation	
	Outputs Consumed or Produced per Period	MRS or MRT	Type of Change	Outputs Consumed or Produced per Period	MRS or MRT
Consumer A	$8a$ and $20b$	$1a = 2b$	Substituting	$7a$ and $23b$	$1a = 2.4b$
Producer α	$16a$ and $5b$	$1a = 3b$	products	$15a$ and $8b$	$1a = 2.4b$

consume and produce, respectively, goods a and b (see Table 2-5). Possibly they are not connected in any way whatsoever. As the numbers indicate for the initial period, α must certainly sell a to others besides A, if it sells anything to A at all, and A must get b at least in part from others besides α. From conditions 1 and 2 we are already familiar with the meaning of the marginal rates. Consumer A's MRS is a purely subjective one: he *feels* that at the margin $1a$ gives him as much satisfaction as $2b$. Firm α's MRT is purely objective: it *knows* that at the margin $1a$ costs as much in resources as $3b$.

Since in our case the fifth condition is originally violated, let us suppose that α is persuaded to change the direction of its production. Instead of using its resources to make $16a$ and $5b$, it uses the same quantity of resources in the next period to make less a and more b, as indicated. There is now 1 less a and there are 3 more b in the economy. If consumer A were to receive, as is possible, 1 less a and 3 more b, he would end up with $7a$ and $23b$. He would be *better off*, for his original MRS indicated that he would be equally well off with 1 less a and only 2 more b. Of course, he might in fact get only 2 more b, but then someone else somewhere could get 1 more b and experience an increase in economic welfare. In short, *the economy should produce more of those goods that are subjectively valued more highly than they objectively cost.* In our case each b is valued by A as much as $\frac{1}{2}$ a, but it only costs, in terms of resources, as much as $\frac{1}{3}$ a.

Clearly, this process should be carried on as far as any divergence in the marginal rates allows. As usual, we have assumed the optimum to have been reached through the working of the principles of diminishing marginal utility for A and increasing marginal cost for α.

Referring to what has been noted earlier, we can state that the fifth marginal condition demands equality of the slopes at the points of actual consumption or production of indifference and production possibility curves. Alternatively, it requires equality, for any set of consumer and producer consuming and producing two given goods, of relative marginal utilities and marginal costs.

$$\left(\frac{MU_a}{MU_b}\right)_A = \left(\frac{MC_a}{MC_b}\right)_\alpha$$

The *sixth marginal condition* is to assure the *optimum degree of input utilization:*

> The marginal rate of substitution between input, x, and real income, a, for any consumer A, who is the supplier of the input, must be the same as the marginal rate of transformation of input, x, into output, a, for any producer, α.

$$MRS^A_{x,a} = MRT^\alpha_{x,a}$$

Table 2-6.

	Initial Situation			Final Situation	
	Input Used and Output Received per Period	MRS or MRT	Type of Change	Input Used and Output Received per Period	MRS or MRT
Consumer A (Supplier of x)	$8x$ and $30a$	$1x = 2a$	Substitution of leisure for product	$9x$ and $33a$	$1x = 2.4a$
Producer α	$119x$ and $315a$	$1x = 3a$		$120x$ and $318a$	$1x = 2.4a$

We now look at consumer A (Table 2-6) in his role as the owner of input x. (Note that in the case of collectively owned inputs we can still conceive of A as being, for instance, the government.) He originally supplies in each period $8x$, receiving in payment, that is, as his real income, part of the product he helps produce, here 30*a*. This consumer is conceived as being able to *subjectively* evaluate the use of *x* and receipt of *a*. In his judgment, it would be "worth" it to supply 1 more *x*, if he were to be compensated by receipt of 2 more *a*. The loss of satisfaction from working one more hour (marginal disutility of labor), for example, is offset by the gain of higher real income (marginal utility of good *a*). Clearly, as before, this subjective evaluation will change with circumstances and, after some time, only increased additions of real income *a* will call forth further equal units of *x*. The increasing marginal disutility of labor, for example, will have to be compensated with increasingly higher additions to real income, which is itself subject to the "law" of diminishing marginal utility. The payment of overtime pay is a case in point.

On the other hand, we have a producer who happens to use the same input, *x* (and others, of course), producing the same product, *a*. The meaning of the MRT, which is an *objective technical* rate, has already been discussed in connection with condition 3 above. The producer is *capable*, by increasing the use of *x* by 1, to increase the output of *a* by 3. Paid to *A*, it would be more than enough to elicit the increased supply of 1*x*. By reducing leisure in favor of use of *x* in this way, consumer *A* is better off, since he would have been equally well off with 9*x* supplied and 32*a* received in return. In short, *whenever leisure is valued less than the output foregone for it, leisure should be reduced.* In our case, the leisure of 1*x* was deemed by *A* worth 2 units of *a*, but the objective sacrifice of output by not using 1*x* was 3*a*.

As always, such substitution should be carried forward as long as it can increase economic welfare. In our case the principles of diminishing marginal utility and diminishing marginal physical product are deemed to have worked and exhausted all possibilities of further gain in the final situation depicted in Table 2-6.

Using the concepts of elementary theory, we might state the sixth condition as demanding equality of the slopes, at the relevant points of operation, of the firm's production function relating *x* to *a*, and the consumer's indifference curve, relating supply of *x* to receipt of *a*. The former has already been identified as the marginal physical product of *x* in making *a* (see condition 3). The meaning of the latter can easily be seen. If the MRS of *A* is 1*x* =

2a, he is saying that the ratio of marginal utility of a to marginal disutility of x equals $\frac{1}{2}$.

$$MRS^A_{x,a} = \left(\frac{MU_a}{MDU_x}\right)A = \frac{1}{2}$$

Only because the utility gained from each a is at the margin half of the utility lost from supplying another x, does A require $2a$ to supply another x. Fulfilling the sixth condition can thus be written as

$$\left(MPP_x{}^a\right)_\alpha = \left(\frac{MDU_x}{MU_a}\right)A$$

The *seventh marginal condition* is to bring about the *optimum allocation of goods over time under conditions of certainty*:

> The marginal rate of substitution between quantities of good a available now, a_t, and available for certain in the future, a_{t+1}, must be the same for any two consumers, A and B, possessing both quantities of good a which are available now and with certainty in the future.

$$MRS^A_{a_t, a_{t+1}} = MRS^B_{a_t, a_{t+1}}$$

We suppose that, to begin with, Consumer A (Table 2-7) owns $40a$, 10 of which are already in his hand at time t, 30 others being due for delivery at some future date, $t + 1$. B is in a similar situation. The MRS indicate again the *subjective* evaluations by the two consumers of the relative worth of good a now versus good a in the future. Consumer A would feel equally well off had he $1a$ more now at the expense of having $2a$ less in the future or vice versa. Yet consumer B makes a different subjective evaluation, equating $1a_t$ with $3a_{t+1}$. At the margin, A clearly, in the original situation, values future a relatively more than does B. To A, each a_{t+1} is worth $\frac{1}{2}a_t$, to B it is worth $\frac{1}{3}a_t$. As has been discussed in connection with condition 1 above, efficiency requires that *those for whom a good is relatively more useful get more of it*. In this case, therefore, A should get more a_{t+1}, for example, by *lending* presently available a_t to get more future a_{t+1}.

Table 2-7

	Initial Situation		Type of Change	Final Situation	
	Quantities Possessed	MRS		Quantities Possessed	MRS
Consumer A (Lender of a_t)	$10a_t$ and $30a_{t+1}$	$1a_t = 2a_{t+1}$	Lending and borrowing under certainty	$9a_t$ and $32a_{t+1}$	$1a_t = 2.6a_{t+1}$
Consumer B (Borrower of a_t)	$7a_t$ and $15a_{t+1}$	$1a_t = 3a_{t+1}$		$8a_t$ and $13a_{t+1}$	$1a_t = 2.6a_{t+1}$
	$17a_t$ and $45a_{t+1}$			$17a_t$ and $45a_{t+1}$	

Suppose that such exchange takes place. At time t, A hands to B $1a_t$, receiving a claim on $2a_{t+1}$ from B in return. A's present consumption of a is reduced, his future consumption raised. The opposite holds for B. In our example, A is equally well off, but B is *better off*. B would have been willing to give up $3a_{t+1}$ for $1a_t$, he had to give up only $2a_{t+1}$. Any rate of exchange for $1a_t$ from $2a_{t+1}$ to $3a_{t+1}$ would have increased efficiency. This will continue to be true until, as in our example, the two MRS have become equal. The principle of diminishing marginal utility will bring this about. As the quantity of a_{t+1} in the hands of A increases and the quantity of a_t falls, the relative value he places on a_{t+1} will fall. It used to be $0.5a_t$, it ended up as $0.38a_t$. B, on the other hand, for analogous reasons, now values each a_{t+1} more than before.

Since the original MRS for A was $1a_t = 2a_{t+1}$, he claimed in fact that his ratio of marginal utility of a_{t+1} to marginal utility of a_t was $\frac{1}{2}$.

$$MRS^A_{a_t, \, a_{t+1}} = \left(\frac{MUa_{t+1}}{MUa_t}\right)_A = \frac{1}{2}$$

Only because the extra satisfaction gained from each a_{t+1} was half that of a_t, was A willing to substitute indifferently $2a_{t+1}$ for $1a_t$. (This rate of indifferent substitution is graphically expressed by the slope of an indifference curve.) Fulfilling the seventh condition, therefore, assures that

$$\left(\frac{MUa_t}{MUa_{t+1}}\right)_A = \left(\frac{MUa_t}{MUa_{t+1}}\right)_B$$

B. Summary

Although economists have traditionally described the Pareto optimum with the help of the above *seven* marginal conditions, it will not have escaped the attentive reader that one could without difficulty find others. In fact, there is a vast number of them. On the other hand, one could also argue that, in a very general sense, there is really only *one* such condition. It can be stated as follows, and its fulfillment assures efficiency throughout the economy.

1. Whenever one can technically transform (through market exchange or within the process of production) one variable into another, the rate of indifferent substitution (the amount of one variable which can be substituted for a unit of the other without feeling of gain or loss) must equal the rate of technical substitution (the amount of one variable which can be obtained objectively by giving up a unit of the other).

2. All equivalent ratios of technical and indifferent substitution must be equal.

3. As long as such marginal inequalities persist, it pays to make changes.

It can be seen that all of our marginal conditions discussed above easily fit this general prescription. Proposition 1 applies to marginal conditions 5 and 6 above. All other marginal conditions are covered by proposition 2, whether we deal with equivalences of technical rates of transformation (conditions 2, 3, and 4) or of subjective rates of substitution (conditions 1 and 7). Obviously, proposition 3 applies to all.

3

The Goals of Equity and Growth

I. EQUITABLE DISTRIBUTION OF OUTPUT

We now turn to a third major economic goal, the *equitable distribution of output*. We are dealing here with a question of justice, and an extremely elusive one at that. Many might agree that society's real income or output should be distributed equitably, but who is to say what that is to mean? It is exactly this issue that has set aflame many a heart, and many a mind has been led to action on this issue by a sense of injustice. Earlier, when discussing the first marginal condition of economic efficiency, we noted that efficiency is neutral between radically different distributions of output. As long as the *marginal* rates of substitution between goods are equal for all individuals, it does not matter how much of these goods these persons possess. But here we *do* face that question, and find there can be no objectively "correct" answer to it.

Some will suggest that "everyone get what he deserves." But that does not bring us any nearer a solution, for who is to determine desert? Everyone will disagree, if someone else decides it for him, and output will hardly be enough, if everyone decides it for himself! Many societies have in fact solved this problem by saying that everyone should get rewarded in accord with his contribution to production, as measured by his luck in the market place. If society rewards a plumber ten times as much as a writer for a week's work, it is concluded that the former was ten times as meritorious, since he obviously got ten times as much only because he contributed ten times as much. The merit standard so understood, however, ignores that some, such as the old, the sick, the very young, contribute nothing to output and hence should get nothing. In short, it denies love, and it skirts the issue of justice by saying everyone else should get what he does get.

Others have proposed that "everyone get what he needs." The communist ideal, "from each according to his ability, to each according to his need," is a special case of this proposition. This approach leads us into just as many difficulties. Who is to determine need? As our introductory discussion of human wants has shown, if we equate needs and wants, this approach denies the reality of scarcity, the fact that everyone according to his ability could not produce enough. If, however, only some wants are to be classified as "true needs," others perhaps as "luxuries," who is to make that classification?

Some, especially socialists, have suggested that needs be considered as equal for all; hence output is *equitably* distributed and welfare maximized, if it is *equally* distributed. Their argument goes something like this. Suppose we consider the distribution of a given output, consisting of fixed quantities of millions of goods. Let us take the prices of these goods and hold them temporarily fixed. Then we can evaluate the millions of quantities and consider the output as a homogeneous quantity, say $600 billion. If we distribute a money income of $600 billion, people will be able to turn it into real income by buying exactly the output produced, no more and no less. If there are 600 million people in this society, everybody should get $1,000. If this were not so, economic welfare or utility would not be maximized. Let us just consider two persons, A and B, and the distribution of $2,000 between them. Both will derive utility from income. It is reasonable to assume that their total utility will rise with rising income, as line 0U in Figure 3-1. No one, of course, would claim to be actually able to *measure* satisfaction in units of utility, but we can *conceive* of the existence of such a unit. Similarly, it is quite likely that the principle of diminishing marginal utility, which we met when discussing the marginal conditions of efficiency, applies to money

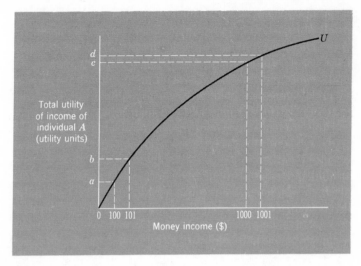

Figure 3-1. (The distance from 100 to 101 and from 1000 to 1001 on the horizontal axis has been exaggerated to facilitate understanding of the argument.)

income as well. A single dollar will probably mean a lot less to Mr. *A* when he has a yearly income of a million than when he has one of $10,000. This is indicated by the curvature of 0*U*. Each additional dollar of income increases *A's total* utility, but successively by less and less. In the figure, an increase of income by $1 from a base of $100 increases total utility by *ab,* from a base of $1,000 by *cd.* Extra or marginal utility *cd* is less than *ab.* Hence we can imagine deriving a curve of marginal utility, as in Figure 3-2. The fact that 0*e* is smaller than 0*f* shows what we have just seen, namely, that the extra utility of a dollar is smaller at a higher ($1000) than at a lower ($100) income. In fact, 0*f* equals *ab* and 0*e* equals *cd.* The *total* utility derived by *A* from any income can now be seen in two ways. It is the *height* of the 0*U* line in Figure 3-1, such as 0*c* showing the total utility of $1000. It also is the *area* under the *MU* line in Figure 3-2, such as 0*ghi* showing the same total utility of $1000. This must be so, since we can imagine the *MU* line to be made up of a multitude of thin columns, each less tall than the previous one and each measuring the extra utility from adding another dollar. Clearly, adding the *extra* utility

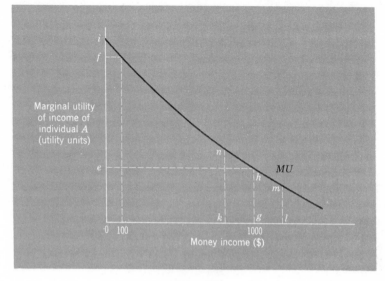

Figure 3-2.

derived from the first, second, third . . . and one-thousandth
dollar gives us the total utility of the first 1,000 dollars.

*If we could be certain that the total and hence the marginal
utility curves of income are the same for all individuals,* we could
easily see why income *equality* would maximize society's total
utility. Equality of income would then imply equality of marginal
utilities of income, such as *gh* for all who have $1000 incomes.
Any deviation from this position would *reduce* total well-being.
Giving *gl* of income to *B*, after taking *gk* = *gl* away from *A*,
would decrease *A*'s total utility by *ghnk*, but increase *B*'s by less,
glmh. Put differently, any inequality of income would then imply
unequal marginal utilities and the possibility for increasing total
utility from a given total income.

But we cannot be certain that individuals are alike in this
fashion. We certainly have no way of measuring this. Hence it
almost seems that we have created a perfect argument for income
inequality. If different individuals' marginal utility curves of income differ, utility in society can be maximized, as it is by
equalizing marginal utilities, only if incomes are unequal. This can

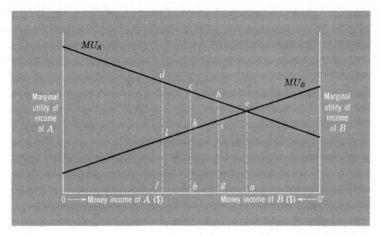

Figure 3-3.

be seen in Figure 3-3. As in Figure 3-2, *A*'s marginal utility of income is measured from origin 0 against possible levels of money income, yielding curve MU_A. Let us suppose that *B*'s marginal utility at any income level is lower, though it also is declining with rising income. *B* simply is a different person with a different, and in this case lower, ability to enjoy income. We could draw an MU_B curve that is, for example, parallel to, but lower than, MU_A. It is more useful, however, to use a different technique. We denote the total money income to be distributed between *A* and *B* by the distance 0 0', then measuring the income in the hands of *B* from 0' towards 0 and his MU_B correspondingly with respect to origin 0'. In this case, it is immediately clear that total utility of *A* and *B* is maximized if *A* gets 0*a* and *B* 0'*a* of income. At that point of income inequality their marginal utilities of income are equal. Maximum welfare is achieved because *that person who can enjoy income relatively more,* here *A, gets more of it.* Any movement away from *a* would reduce total utility. If we gave more income to *B* at the expense of *A,* as seen from the area under the curves, *B* would gain less than *A* would lose. If we gave more income to *A* at the expense of *B, A* would gain less than *B* would lose. Here is one way of giving to everyone "according to his needs." Yet needs, as measured by the marginal utility of income, cannot *in fact* be measured. And it is this inability to measure what is conceptually clear enough, which provides the final impetus for the argument for equality of incomes.

Suppose that we equalized incomes in our example, A receiving 0*b* and B the same, 0′*b*. *If we knew* the *MU* curves as drawn, total utility would clearly not be maximized at that position. An extra dollar would add more to A's than a dollar less would take away from B's satisfaction. We should move towards *a*. But we *don't* know the comparative level of the curves. Point *a* might in fact coincide with *b*, if MU_b were higher intersecting MU_A at *c* rather than *e*. In this case we would maximize utility by doing nothing to alter the equal income distribution. Point *a* might instead coincide with *f*, if MU_b were still higher relatively to MU_A, intersecting it at *d* rather than *e*. In this case, we would maximize utility by redistributing income from A to B. If incomes are equally distributed, such as at *b*, there is thus an equal chance for the true maximum, here *a*, to be to the right or left of this point, that is, for total utility to be increased by raising the income of A at the expense of B's or vice versa. Hence any deviation from income equality makes it equally likely that we go in the right or the wrong direction. If we moved in the right direction, in our diagram towards 0′ from *b*, assuming the impossible, namely, that the curves of *MU* are known, total utility would be raised. Going from *b* to *g* alone would raise A's utility by *bghc*, lower B's by only *bgik*, bringing a net gain to society of *kihc*. If we moved in the wrong direction, in our diagram from *b* towards 0, which we are equally likely to do, since we in fact do *not* know the *MU* curves involved, total utility would be lowered. Going from *b* to *f*, where *bf = bg* in size, would raise B's utility by *fbkl*, lower A's by *fbcd*, causing a net loss to society of *lkcd*. The *occurrence* of a loss or gain in total utility is equally probable, but the probable *size* of a loss is always larger than the probable size of a gain, given any deviation from equality. Area *lkcd* exceeds area *kihc*. Thus the calculus of probability comes to the aid of those desiring an equal income distribution. Large-scale deviations from the rule of equality, they argue, would involve a *certain* social loss.

This is saying, in a way, that, in the absence of any *proof* to the contrary, we might just as well assume that all men are alike in their ability to enjoy income. This clearly strikes a receptive cord in the hearts of those who favor political democracy. That system also assumes that men are alike in many ways, at least so far as their endowment with intelligence and ability to use it is concerned. Why else would one want to give an equal vote to each man? Now in the economic realm, there would be similar equality when voting for the use of resources with equally powerful incomes that can be spent.

Yet we should not be blind to the possible criticisms of this position. These are many. The equating of money and real income, for example, causes trouble when relative prices change. Another criticism concerns the possibility of *rising* marginal utility of income with increases in income. However, the most serious one is undoubtedly concerned with the question of incentives. It might just be that the given type of income distribution is closely interrelated with a society's ability to use resources efficiently and to make output grow over time. If high incomes in the hands of some, for instance, were necessary to assure faster growth or to bring forth achievements that would otherwise remain undone, insistence on equality would be akin to the action of a greedy child who, trying to grab more pie than he should, spills some on the floor, causing all to have less altogether. Is it not worth some inequality, some would argue, if without it we cannot have a Michelangelo or a Newton or a Beethoven, or if without it we, as well as our children, will have less of everything?

We are back at the point of our beginning. Though we can recognize the problem, we do not have a clear answer. Surely there is some minimum need, however impossible to define, below which nobody's real income can go. Similarly, we cannot neglect entirely the principle of rewarding factors according to merit, if we want to keep them functioning and bringing forth their best. Somewhere within this field of tension between perfect equality and glaring inequality, we must choose. Need sets a limit to inequality, incentive to equality.

II. SUFFICIENT GROWTH OF OUTPUT

Finally, we come to the goal of *growth of output over time.* This is a dynamic question. We have talked about the full and efficient use of *given* resources, and about an equitable distribution of output so produced. Now we must talk about how the given quantities can be *changed*. Again we have before us an idea that is clearly meaningful, yet equally hard to define. Nobody can fail to be impressed by the dramatic difference between the tradition-ridden societies of some time back and the modern industrial nations now occupying the same space on the surface of the earth. Progress certainly is *the* watchword of this century, and more change is now occurring in the lifetime of a man than over many centuries before. In many areas of the world, economic growth is occurring; that is, *output per man is rising* rapidly. Where it is not, great efforts are being made to achieve this goal by increasing the quantities and qualities of labor, land, and capital and by changing radically the environments within which they are being used. Some of us may have a longing for those "good old days" that seem to have supported so much more stable and leisurely and secure lives. Yet a visit to the less-developed world today can vividly demonstrate to us even now the smells and filth and inconveniences of the past and make us long for the cleanliness and wealth of modern times. Though there is much lacking in man's spiritual progress, his economic progress is undeniable, and most of mankind would want to have it no other way. We may admit sorrowfully that man's ability to produce so much more so much more easily has given him more power than he has learned to handle. Not only can he build a life of bliss, but also a life of terror and war on a scale unheard of in the history of mankind. But we must be realistic. There is no reversing man's decision to follow the path of economic growth.

The only real questions is: At what rate do we want this progress to occur? Should output—and with it our ability to do good or evil—grow at a rate of 2% per year, or 5%, or 12%? Here again, reasonable men may reasonably differ. There certainly is some maximum rate of growth beyond which we cannot go. Whatever we do involves the sacrifice of something else that might have been done instead. If we train more teachers and doctors to improve the quality of our labor force, we are sacrificing the food that teachers and doctors and students might have produced during this time of their mental and physical improvement. If we use men and equipment to "mine" magnesium from the sea, we cannot use them to build homes. If we build roads and factories and machines, we cannot use the inputs involved to make refrigerators instead. If we channel resources into improving our technical know-how, the organization of production, or the administration of our economy, they cannot be used to make clothing at the same time. Yet all these things must be done for growth to occur. Clearly, there is an irreducible minimum of food alone that a society must grow, and of clothing and shelter that it must provide, before it can even think of doing anything else. Depending on how close to this minimum the production of physical necessities for survival can be and is depressed, resources are released for growth. This question could be decided "by accident" through the actions of millions of individuals following their own desires; it can be entirely decided by a powerful and dictatorial government, by the conscious choice of a majority in a democratic ballot, or in other ways. There is no objective answer to the question of how much present sacrifice potential future bliss is worth.

4

Perfectly Competitive Capitalism

It is now time to ask exactly how an economic system might be organized to attempt to achieve the four goals enumerated in the two previous chapters. Since, at least in the West, so much of the economic theory of socialism has its roots in the study of the capitalist economic order, we shall begin our task in this chapter by considering, as briefly as possible and necessary, the most famous blueprint of capitalism, the perfectly competitive economy.

I. THE CONDITIONS

We shall consider a simplified world in which there are only two groups of actors. These are, first, *households* which privately own all factors of production, selling the services of labor, land, and capital to firms, and using the income so received to buy the outputs of firms. Secondly, *firms* buy inputs from households and sell their products to households. This basic relationship is most simply illustrated with the circular flow diagram of Figure 4-1. It shows clearly why the capitalist economy is often referred to as a *market* economy. It is not under the direction of any central authority. Its organization consists solely of voluntary exchanges undertaken by households and firms in the marketplace. There are two types of market, the goods market in which the output of commodities and services is supplied by firms and demanded by households, and the factor market in which households supply the services of productive resources and firms

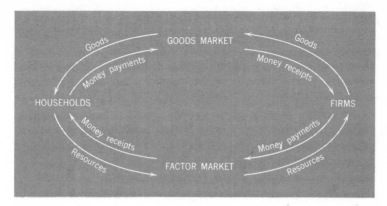

Figure 4-1.

demand them. All this activity is *coordinated by prices* of goods and factors.

More specifically, we assume that households own resources and firms produce products that are *homogeneous and* easily *mobile.* The services of labor, land, or capital can not only be divided into any (homogeneous) units of quantity desired, but they can also easily and swiftly be shifted from one occupation to another or from one geographic location to another. No firm has any reason to prefer the resource of one seller over that of another so far as quality is concerned. There are no restraints of any kind that would prevent resource owners from having them used where their employment would bring the highest price. Firms produce homogeneous products in any one market, hence no buyer of goods has any reason either to prefer any particular seller over another. Firms can supply whatever, whenever, and wherever they wish, thus selling any good at the highest price they can get for it. There are also no restrictions on households' demand for goods and firms' demand for inputs. Each can buy wherever the price is lowest.

Furthermore, we assume that all households and firms possess *complete knowledge* of the economy. Any discrepancies in prices between sellers of goods or factors will immediately be known; hence in the market for any one good or factor such discrepancies will rapidly be eliminated.

This will happen because we assume that the motivating force for the behavior of households is to *maximize their well-being*; thus they will buy goods at the lowest price possible and sell inputs to the highest bidder. At the same time, firms are assumed to *maximize profits* for their owners; hence they will also buy resources at the lowest and sell goods at the highest price.

Finally we assume that in all goods and factor markets the number of buyers and sellers is so large that *no single buyer or seller by his own action can appreciably influence the prevailing price.*

II. THE MARKETS

What prices actually will be, however, will depend on the outcome of the competitive struggle in which all participants, following their self-interest, aim at the payment of low and the receipt of high prices. Clearly, no price in any market can be maintained for long unless the quantities supplied and demanded at that price are equal. If quantity supplied exceeded quantity demanded, sellers would bid against each other, lowering the price. If quantity supplied fell short of that demanded, buyers would bid up the price. In both cases, this would continue until the lower or higher price had sufficiently changed the desires to buy and sell as to bring them into equality. Figure 4-2 shows the situation in the *goods market* in detail. Part *a* depicts the demand of a single buyer for a good for a given period. Given all other factors that might influence it, this demand is shown by *dd*. The lower the price of the good, the greater is the quantity of it that the household would be willing to buy. Obviously this reflects the operation of the principle of diminishing marginal utility, which we have met before. Since the subjective value of a unit of a good is likely to decline as larger quantities of it are possessed, a household, given any price, will buy only a limited quantity of it. At a price of $1, he will buy only 7 units, for example, if the next one is deemed to add to satisfaction an amount not considered "worth" the $1 price. It might, however, be considered "worth" 90¢, and at a price of 90¢ the eighth unit might be bought.

Part *c* depicts the supply by a single firm of the same good for a given period. Given all other factors that might influence it, the supply is shown by *ss*. The higher the price of the good, the greater is the quantity of it that the firm would be willing to supply. This reflects the operation of the principle of increasing marginal costs, which we have also met. Certainly, in the short run some of the firm's inputs, such as buildings and equipment, will be fixed, and it might be able to increase output only by varying some, but not all, inputs, such as materials and labor. This will eventually call into operation the principle of diminishing marginal physical product, implying increasing marginal costs. If each additional unit of a variable input brings successively smaller and smaller additions to output (diminishing marginal physical product), equal increases in output will require successively larger increases in inputs (increasing marginal cost). This cost can obviously be measured not only in real resource units but also in dollars. If plotted, the dollar marginal cost curve gives us (with a slight qualification irrelevant here) the supply curve of the firm, showing for each quantity to be supplied the minimum price the firm must receive. If the marginal cost of producing 190 units is $1, the firm will at most supply 190 units at a price of $1. If marginal cost is rising, higher output will involve a marginal cost of more, and unless price rises the firm will not produce another unit adding to its cost, say, $1.10 while only adding to its revenue $1. We have met here the familiar rule of profit maximization or loss minimization which occurs when the extra (marginal) revenue of selling one more unit just equals the extra (marginal) cost of producing it.

Parenthetically let us note that the actual *size* of the firm's profit (or loss) depends, of course, on its *total* cost as related to its *total* revenue. In our example, total revenue is 190 units times the $1 price (or average revenue), or $190. If the firm's *average* cost curve, showing the ratio of total cost to quantity produced at each conceivable quantity of output, is given by *AC*, we can find the total cost as 190 units times the 90¢ average cost, or $171. Hence profit is $19 (190 units times 10¢ average profit). For the reader not familiar with the theory of the firm, it might be added that average costs may well fall over some range of conceivable outputs, as it does in Figure 4-2*c*, because, among other things,

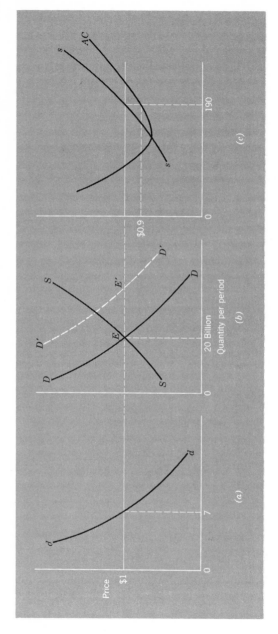

Figure 4-2. The goods market. (*a*) Single household. (*b*) All households and firms. (*c*) Single firm.

the fixed costs, such as for the buildings and equipment in our case, are spread out over more and more units as output is raised. Eventually, however, rising marginal costs will overpower this tendency and pull up average costs.

We can now imagine an aggregate market demand curve to be derived by horizontally adding at each price those of individual buyers. This is shown as *DD* in Figure 4-2*b*. The horizontal scale of part *b* is, of course, quite different from that of parts *a* and *c*. Similarly, we can imagine a horizontal summation of individual firms' supply curves resulting in the aggregate market supply curve *SS*. As it happens, $1 is the only price that clears the market, as in the aggregate at this price the same quantity of our good is supplied as demanded, namely, 20 billion units.

As a result, the supply curve *to the single buyer* will appear to look like the horizontal line in part *a*. Price to the single buyer is a *parameter* he cannot change by himself. He might, because of a change in taste, demand twice as much at any price as before (shifting *dd* parallel to the right), yet *DD* in part *b* would only shift right so inappreciably that the equilibrium market price would remain at $1.

On the other hand, the demand curve *to the single firm* will appear as the solid horizontal line in part *c*. Price to the single firm is also a parameter that it cannot change by itself. It might, because of a change in technology, supply twice as much at any price as before (shifting *ss* parallel to the right and *AC* down), yet *SS* in part *b* would only shift right so inappreciably that the equilibrium market price would remain at $1.

Yet if many or all consumers desired more of this good, the many tiny effects on *DD* would add to a noticeable shift, such as to *D'D'*, raising the price appreciably. As a result, the demand curves *as they appear to individual firms* would shift up in part *c*, causing each firm to supply more along *ss*. The aggregate effect of this is, of course, seen in part *b* as a movement along *SS* to the intersection with *D'D'*. Given some time, new firms, attracted by the profits in this line of activity, might spring up, causing also *SS* to shift right, and lowering the long-run equilibrium price. This in a nutshell is the principle of consumer sovereignty. Consumers, like kings, want more of a good, and they get more.

Prices are the signals, and the profit motive is the driving force of this change.

Figure 4-3 will serve to illustrate the same principles for the *factor market*. Part *a* depicts the supply of a single seller of a resource for a given period. Given all other factors that might influence it, this supply is shown by *ss*. The higher the price of a resource, the greater the quantity of it that a household would be willing to offer. This reflects the principle of increasing marginal disutility or alternative opportunities forgone. The more hours of labor are supplied, for example, the scarcer becomes leisure and the more each minute of it is deemed to be "worth." Until 8 units of labor are supplied per period, the leisure so lost may be considered worth less than the $1 per unit of labor received. Thereafter, leisure might be considered worth more and would be sacrificed only for a higher price.

Part *c* depicts the demand for this resource for a given period by a single firm in *dd*. The lower the price of the resource, the greater is the quantity which the firm is willing to buy. This again reflects the operation of the principle of diminishing marginal physical product. As new potential units of labor are added, for example, to other fixed inputs, the extra output produced by each extra unit of labor declines. Given the price of the product, the extra revenue obtainable from each extra labor unit declines also. No firm, desiring to maximize profits, will pay more to an extra unit of input than is added to the firm's revenue by the employment of that unit. Hence the maximum amount payable to an input declines with increased use of that input as shown by *dd*. Given the $1 price, our firm will buy no more than 32 units of the input in question.

Part *b* is constructed like Figure 4-2*b* by horizontally summing the individual household's input supply curves and the firms' input demand curves. $1 happens to be the only price clearing the market and equating aggregate demand and supply for this input at a level of 6 million units per period.

The demand curve *to the single seller* will, therefore, look like the horizontal line in Figure 4-3*a*. Price again appears as a parameter that cannot be changed by him alone. If for any reason, the single household were to supply twice as much of a

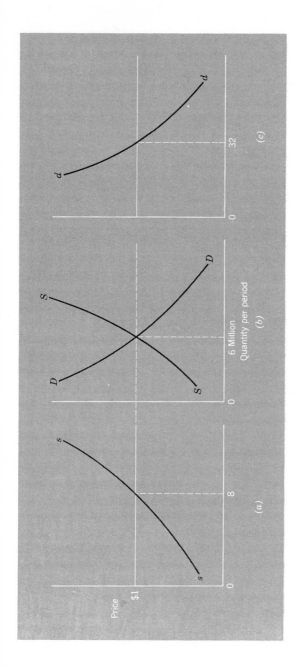

Figure 4-3. The factor market. (*a*) Single household. (*b*) All households and firms. (*c*) Single firm.

given input (shifting *ss* parallel to the right), SS in part *b* would not shift appreciably enough to lower price.

Similarly, the supply curve *to the single firm* will appear as the horizontal line in part *c*. It is a price taker in the factor market also. An improvement in technology may, for instance, raise the marginal physical productivity of an input, shifting *dd* up; yet *DD* would not be affected enough to raise the equilibrium input price.

Yet if *all* households were to increase the supply of this input, SS *would* shift strongly, the price would fall and each firm would find it profitable to use more. Again the economic system would have accommodated the desires of the consumers, here in their role as the suppliers of productive resources.

III. THE PRICE SYSTEM

So far we have only looked at one part of the system at a time. Surely, however, it will have become obvious to the reader that no single change can occur by itself. It will have widespread repercussions and in a real sense affect everything else in the economy. Any single shift in demand between two goods, for example, will call forth a change in production not only of two, but of all goods. More will be produced where demand has risen, less where it has fallen. This will immediately cause higher demand for the resources needed for the former, and lower demand for those used in the production of the latter. This will most likely change absolute and relative factor prices, and hence absolute and relative incomes, since the income of any household depends on the quantities of inputs it offers and the prices it gets for them. The change in factor prices will cause all firms to reassess their most profitable factor combination used, while the change in household incomes will thoroughly alter the pattern of demand for almost all goods. Finally, we can conceive of a new equilibrium being established, but very few quantities will be equal to what they were before.

It is quite possible to conceive of this interdependence in the economy as a set of millions of simultaneous equations which has to be solved anew after each change upsets an imaginary equilibrium. Theoretically, these equations could express the conditions of demand and supply of goods and factors and could be solved for the one unique set of equilibrium prices which would equate demand and supply for each good and factor of production. Assuming that households wanted to maximize their utility and firms their profits, one could conceive of myriad demand equations expressing households' and firms' demands for goods and factors, respectively, under all conceivable circumstances. Similarly, the supply equations could express households' and firms' supplies of factors and goods, respectively, under all conceivable circumstances. Such a system has in fact been written down, in a very general form, by Walras and is often referred to as the "Walrasian system of general equilibrium." [1] In reality, however, we must realize that even today there is no computer even in sight which could solve fast enough such a system of equations, even if this information could be gathered in a central place, as it cannot. This is the remarkable work of the price system in a capitalist market economy, where economics comes to the aid of mathematics and competition in free markets solves by trial and error what cannot be solved in any other way.

IV. THE LEVEL OF EMPLOYMENT

How well, let us ask then, would such a system fulfill the major economic goals discussed in the previous chapters? Considering first the question of *full employment of resources,* we have to decide, of course, what we wish to mean by that term. Let us suppose we did define full employment, as suggested in Chapter 2, as the state of affairs where resources are used at the rate desired by their owners. As we have seen in Figure 4-3, this rate may vary with the price paid for the use of resources, but the only equilibrium price possible is the one equating the quantities of a resource supplied and demanded in the aggregate. We clearly can never, in a perfectly competitive economy, have unemployment and equilibrium at the same time. Unemployment, the situation where a smaller quantity of a resource is used than offered for use by its owners, would exist if the price were

---

[1] See the English translation, Léon Walras, *Elements of Pure Economics* (Homewood, Illinois: Richard D. Irwin, 1954).

above equilibrium or if supply exceeded demand. There would, therefore, be a tendency in the presence of unemployment for resource prices to fall. Would that eliminate unemployment?

Looking at this from the standpoint of a single firm, the answer might seem to be clearly in the affirmative. As the price of any input is declining, we have seen in Figure 4-3c, it would be in the self-interest of the producer to hire more of this input. Any *single* firm could hope to increase its profit by producing more in this way and selling the extra output at an *unchanged* price. Yet if all firms do the same thing for the same reason, the price of the *product* will fall and the original fall in the factor price *relative to* the product price may have been offset, eliminating the incentive to produce more and hire more of the input. Then the factor price would have to fall all over again.

Yet again it would seem from the standpoint of a *single* firm that unemployment will still be cured, for with product prices falling people can afford to buy more. This neglects the fact that with factor prices *money incomes* have also fallen.

It has, however, been argued that even if factor and goods prices fall together, they will fall relative to an *unchanged* quantity of money in the economy the size of which is determined by monetary authorities. Whoever is holding this money will find that its real purchasing power is continually rising and this will make people eventually feel so rich that they will spend more on that account. Their real income may be the same, but their real wealth is rising, hence eventually increasing the demand for goods in all markets, increasing output and the employment of inputs. Or instead, if demand does not rise originally, prices being lower, less money is needed to buy the output; with the stock of money unchanged, people will try to get rid of it by buying securities which will drive down interest rates and encourage a rise in demand for capital goods. This, indeed, may be true, but how long will it take? This is a practical question that we cannot answer. If such mechanism were to work swiftly, unemployment in the competitive system might be no problem at all. If, however, an unemployment disequilibrium could not cure itself except by 30 years of continually falling prices of factors and products, we might not be too content with the performance of this economy.

V. THE DEGREE OF EFFICIENCY

Let us suppose for the moment that a full employment equilibrium does exist. How well would the competitive economy do with respect to *economic efficiency?* Here, indeed, it would perform admirably well.

Following their self-interest, all the actors in our economy would in fact bring about the fulfillment of all conceivable marginal conditions of efficiency. Let us see why.

Each consumer would maximize the satisfaction received from his money income, if he spent it in such a way that the marginal utility received from a dollar's worth of any good is the same for all goods he buys. If he can purchase, for instance, good a at a price of $2 per unit (P_a), and good b at a price of $7 per unit (P_b), he would be very unwise to buy quantities of a and b such that the satisfaction of the marginal unit of $a(MU_a)$ is the same as that of $b(MU_b)$. If he were in that position, he could clearly buy one unit less of b, saving $7, one unit more of a, losing $2, and leave his total satisfaction unchanged while spending $5 less than before. As a result, MU_a will fall, and MU_b will rise, as he has more of a and less of b. Only when $MU_a/P_a = MU_b/P_b$ will he have gotten the most out of his income. Any further switch will not improve his position. He might buy another dollar's worth of a, but it would then only raise his satisfaction by as much as the loss incurred when he bought a dollar's worth less of b. This of course, must hold for all his purchases, and we can expand the above expression to n goods by writing that a consumer maximizes his satisfaction from spending his income if

$$\frac{MU_a}{P_a} = \frac{MU_b}{P_b} = \frac{MU_c}{P_c} = \cdots \frac{MU_n}{P_n}$$

Although we would not claim that any consumer ever attempts to *measure* the marginal utility to him of any good, in the sense of assigning to it a cardinal number, such as 77.7 utils, we can still argue that satisfaction-maximizing consumers must be doing just that without being particularly conscious of it. Every time he turns over a dollar in his hand, deciding what he wants "most" for it, the consumer is in fact deciding where his marginal utility (extra satisfaction!) is presently highest. Every time he is indifferent between two goods, he is clearly saying that his marginal utilities for the two are equal.

Now it is a simple step to show why in a perfectly competitive world the *first marginal condition* would be automatically fulfilled in equilibrium. Each consumer reaches equilibrium, the state from which he has no desire to deviate, when

$$\frac{MU_a}{MU_b} = \frac{P_a}{P_b}, \quad \text{and} \quad \frac{MU_a}{MU_n} = \frac{P_a}{P_n}, \quad \text{etc.}$$

All prices are the same to all consumers. Hence their marginal utility ratios must be equal, because they are equal to the same price ratios.

$$\left(\frac{MU_a}{MU_b}\right)_A = \frac{P_a}{P_b} = \left(\frac{MU_a}{MU_b}\right)_B$$

There is no need, therefore, for consumers to exchange products with each other, as suggested as a possibility in Chapter 2. They don't even have to be aware of each other's existence. All that matters is that both determine their actions on the basis of the same signals, prices in the competitive market.

The *second marginal condition* would be similarly fulfilled. A firm could only maximize its profit, if for all its products the relation of price to marginal cost were identical, that is,

$$\frac{P_a}{MC_a} = \frac{P_b}{MC_b} = \frac{P_c}{MC_c} = \cdots \frac{P_n}{MC_n}$$

Let us just look at goods a and b. If, for instance $P_a = \$7$ and $P_b = \$19$, while the marginal costs were identical at $7, the firm would be wise to cut output of a by a unit, losing $7 of revenue as well as cost, and using $7 of resources to produce $1b$, bringing $19 of revenue. As a result, with the same total expenditure, revenue, hence profit, could be raised by $12.

If each firm, producing a and b, has the incentive to make the ratio of marginal costs equal to that of prices, and *prices being the same for all producers,* different firms' marginal cost ratios will in fact be identical. The second condition is, therefore, fulfilled.

$$\left(\frac{MC_a}{MC_b}\right)_\alpha = \frac{P_a}{P_b} = \left(\frac{MC_a}{MC_b}\right)_\beta$$

Again, there is no need for firms to know of each other or consciously to cooperate. They have only to follow their self-interest and take the course of action dictated to them by prices.

The *third marginal condition* will be fulfilled out of the same motives. To each firm prices of outputs, such as of good $a(P_a)$, and inputs, such as of input $x(P_x)$, are given. A firm can increase its profit as long as the value of a factor's marginal physical product, that is, $MPP_x{}^a \cdot P_a$, exceeds the price of the input. If a unit of labor costs \$1 (P_x), adds to output $10a$ $(MPP_x{}^a)$, and if each a sells for 15¢ (P_a), it clearly pays to hire the input for \$1 and gain from its activity \$1.50. Hence profit maximization drives firms to the point where $MPP_x{}^a \cdot P_a = P_x$. This can be rewritten as $MPP_x{}^a = P_x/P_a$. Since each firm will strive to do this *and is faced with identical prices,* the firms' marginal physical products must be equal, as demanded by the third marginal condition.

$$\left(MPP_x{}^a \right)_\alpha = \frac{P_x}{P_a} = \left(MPP_x{}^a \right)_\beta$$

We might also note that $P_x/MPP_x{}^a = P_a$ in equilibrium. The left side of this equation is nothing but the marginal cost of a. If $P_x = \$1$ and $1x$, being used alone to make more a, produces $10a$, then the marginal cost of $10a = \$1$ or the marginal cost of $1a = P_x/MPP_x{}^a = \$1/10 = \$0.10$. The third marginal condition thus elaborates upon the second, showing that marginal costs must not only be proportional to, but *equal* to, prices. $MC_a = P_a$, $MC_b = P_b$, etc. This is, of course, the well-known rule of profit maximization in perfect competition, which we have met before.

The third condition also anticipates the fourth. Since $MC_a = P_a$, we can write

$$\frac{MC_a}{MC_a} = \frac{P_a}{P_a}$$

which is also

$$\frac{P_x/MPP_x{}^a}{P_y/MPP_y{}^a} = 1$$

Hence

$$\frac{P_x}{MPP_x{}^a} = \frac{P_y}{MPP_y{}^a} \qquad \text{or} \qquad \frac{P_x}{P_y} = \frac{MPP_x{}^a}{MPP_y{}^a}$$

Hence fulfillment of the third anticipates fulfillment of the fourth.

The *fourth marginal condition* will be fulfilled in a way analogous to the first. Each firm will maximize its output from a given expenditure for resources if and only if the marginal physical product received from a dollar's worth of any resource is the same for all inputs it buys. If it can purchase, for example, input x at a price of \$2 per unit (P_x) and input y at a price of \$6 per unit (P_y), it would be very unwise to use such quantities of x and y that their marginal physical products are equal, say $10a$. In this case, using 1 less y will cut costs by \$6 and output by $10a$, while another \$2 spent on x would restore the old output level and \$6 spent on x would raise it by $20a$. Maximum output with given costs or given output at minimum cost requires that $MPP_x{}^a/P_x = MPP_y{}^a/P_y$, etc. for other inputs. This can be rewritten as $MPP_x{}^a/MPP_y{}^a = P_x/P_y$. Since each firm can only maximize profits if this condition is fulfilled, *and input prices are the same for all firms*, perfect competition will bring about the situation where

$$\left(\frac{MPP_x{}^a}{MPP_y{}^a}\right)_\alpha = \frac{P_x}{P_y} = \left(\frac{MPP_x{}^a}{MPP_y{}^a}\right)_\beta$$

Again there is no need for an actual exchange of inputs between firms as discussed in Chapter 2. Firms, following their own self-interest, will tend to buy the correct quantities of inputs in the first place, guided solely by the market prices involved.

Since the *fifth marginal condition* is a combination of the first and second, we have already shown by implication why and how it will be fulfilled in perfectly competitive equilibrium. Consumers wish to make marginal utility ratios of any two goods equal to their price ratios, firms strive to make marginal cost ratios equal to the *same* price ratios. Hence, whether they know each other or not,

$$\left(\frac{MU_a}{MU_b}\right)_A = \frac{P_a}{P_b} = \left(\frac{MC_a}{MC_b}\right)_\alpha$$

Consumers will adjust their purchases and firms their production volumes until this is true.

The *sixth marginal condition* has been partially touched upon in our discussion of the third. We noticed there that firms would be driven by the profit motive to equate marginal cost with price, or make $P_x/MPP_x{}^a = P_a$. Hence $MPP_x{}^a = P_x/P_a$. Households, as suppliers of inputs, can now be seen driven by the desire to minimize dissatisfaction (disutility) or maximize utility. This is only the case when the marginal disutility from supplying a resource per dollar of resource supplied equals the marginal utility of the real income per dollar of real income. A consumer would obviously not be maximizing his well-being if he purchased good a at a price of \$3 per unit (P_a) and sold resource x at a price of \$6 (P_x), while having equal utility from the former (MU_a) as disutility from the latter (MDU_x). By supplying 1 more x, he would gain \$6, which spent on a, would bring twice as much utility as the supply of x caused disutility. Only when $MDU_x/P_x = MU_a/P_a$, has the consumer done his best. This can be rewritten as $MDU_x/MU_a = P_x/P_a$. *Since P_x and P_a are the same for all households and firms*, the desire to maximize utility or profits assures that

$$\left(\frac{MDU_x}{MU_a}\right)_A = \frac{P_x}{P_a} = \left(MPP_x{}^a\right)_\alpha$$

This, of course, holds for any input, such as y, giving us $MDU_y/MU_a = P_y/P_a$.

Hence it will also be true that

$$\frac{MDU_x/MU_a}{MDU_y/MU_a} = \frac{P_x/P_a}{P_y/P_a} \qquad \text{or} \qquad \frac{MDU_x}{MDU_y} = \frac{P_x}{P_y}$$

that is, marginal disutility ratios of various inputs throughout the economy will be equal to the price ratios of such inputs. In equilibrium, inputs will be used such that for each dollar of income they earn, an equal subjective sacrifice is involved, no matter where the inputs are employed.

Little needs to be said about the *seventh marginal condition*. Our discussion of the first condition applies fully. The same good, a, at two different moments in time, can easily be conceived as two different goods. Substituting a_t for a and a_{t+1} for b in our discussion above, we can show that this condition also will be fulfilled in an equilibrium of perfect competition.

VI. THE RATIONAL PRICE SYSTEM DEFINED

We have now reached a point of our discussion where it is possible to introduce an extremely important concept, namely, that of a *rational price system*. We have seen that in a perfectly competitive equilibrium, the attainment of which lies in the self-interest of households as well as of firms, the following would be true.

1. Prices of goods would be proportional to marginal utilities as well as marginal costs.

2. Prices of factors of production would be proportional to marginal disutilities as well as marginal physical productivities.

For simplicity confining ourselves to two goods (a and b) and two inputs (x and y), statement 1 can be written as

$$\frac{MU_a}{MU_b} = \frac{P_a}{P_b} = \frac{MC_a}{MC_b}$$

Fulfillment of this condition means that a rational price system exists in the goods market. It implies, incidentally, fulfillment of marginal conditions 1, 2, 5, and 7. Relative goods prices reflect relative preferences as well as relative scarcities. Such prices are rational because as guides in our economic behavior they assure efficiency; they also assure the maximum production of satisfaction with the minimum resource cost. For all goods produced the marginal satisfaction attained per dollar of resources used will be the same, that is,

$$\frac{MU_a}{MC_a} = \frac{MU_b}{MC_b} \cdot \cdot \cdot \text{etc.}$$

We cannot change the allocation of resources from one activity to another and increase economic welfare.

Statement 2 can be written as

$$\frac{MDU_x{}^a}{MDU_y{}^a} = \frac{P_x}{P_y} = \frac{MPP_x{}^a}{MPP_y{}^a}$$

Fulfillment of this condition means that a rational price system exists in the factor market. It implies fulfillment of marginal conditions 3, 4, and 6. Relative factor prices reflect relative preferences and relative productivities. Such prices are rational because as guides in our economic behavior they assure efficiency and assure the maximum production of output with a minimum expenditure of dissatisfaction. For all inputs used the marginal output per unit of dissatisfaction will be the same, that is,

$$\frac{MPP_x}{MDU_x} = \frac{MPP_y}{MDU_y} \cdots \text{etc.}$$

We cannot change the use of resources to increase economic welfare.

Hence assuring economic efficiency means advocating a rational price system. A rational price system can be brought about by perfectly competitive conditions in all markets.

VII. THE DISTRIBUTION OF INCOME

As an integral part of the competitive pricing process, factor prices are established. This implies immediately that the *income distribution* is determined. There is not much that one can say about it, except that it is very unlikely that incomes of households will be equal. Those households that possess large quantities of capital and land and who are able to perform labor particularly in demand will undoubtedly have higher incomes than others for whom the reverse is true. Whether an income distribution so established is deemed equitable or not depends on the values of the person involved.

VIII. THE GROWTH OF OUTPUT

A similar situation exists with respect to *economic growth* in a perfectly competitive world. How much of a period's output consists of consumer goods and how much of new capital goods capable of enlarging the capacity to produce, depends on the voluntary decisions of households to spend their incomes on either the former or the latter. Similarly, the owners of firms, spurned on by the relentless competitive struggle, may decide to use some or all of their profits to improve upon their technical know-how. On the other hand, the means of the typical competitive firm may be insufficient to do so on a large enough scale. In any case, it will be up to the individual observer and his judgment whether the growth of output over time which does occur is "sufficient" or not.

5

Capitalist Reality and Socialist Critique

We have seen how our four economic goals might be dealt with in the framework of a perfectly competitive capitalistic economy. Such an economy, however, has never existed. Whatever imperfections the "ideal" might have, those of real capitalist economies in the middle of the 20th century are likely to be worse.

I. THE LIKELIHOOD OF UNEMPLOYMENT

There is not even a hint of an automatic tendency for the achievement of full employment. Because of downward rigidities of prices of goods as well as factors of production, it is quite possible for large-scale unemployment *and* equilibrium to co-exist. That is, it is quite possible for labor, capital, and land *not* to be utilized (although their owners would desire them to be used) and for there to be no tendency for change whatsoever. Modern governments have come to recognize this and are implementing deliberate monetary and fiscal policies to remedy the situation. In a period of depression or threat of it, for example, they may try to stimulate the use of idle resources by stimulating the demand for output through cutting taxes or increasing government spending or making it easier to borrow from the banks.[1]

---

[1] This point is discussed in great detail in Arnold Collery, *National Income and Employment Analysis* in this series, pp. 17–116.

54

II. THE PROBLEM OF INEFFICIENCY

There also is very little in reality corresponding to the competitive ideal of efficiency. The conditions of perfect competition, which we have discussed, typically do *not* pertain in the real world. Mobility of goods and resources is restricted in innumerable ways, goods and resources are not standardized, knowledge of prices and quantities is very imperfect and in fact worsened by deliberate misinformation, and many buyers and sellers are so powerful in their markets that they can and do influence prices by their individual actions. It will be in the self-interest of monopolists to restrict the sale of goods and resources to raise the prices they receive; monopsonists will restrict their purchases of goods and resources to depress the prices they have to pay.[2] As a result, the price system is far from rational and economic inefficiencies abound. Modern governments also recognize that. Through taxes and subsidies and many kinds of legislation (such as antitrust), they could in theory induce or force firms and households to change their behavior so as to better conform to the competitive ideal. But clearly such efforts are hopeless. No government can possibly collect enough information on billions and billions of details, as would be required to correct *all* the imperfections of the actual economy. Most taxes and subsidies are, in fact, introduced for reasons other than the attempt to improve efficiency. To make things worse, it has been shown conclusively[3] that any *piecemeal* fulfillment of the conditions of the Pareto optimum may not increase welfare at all! The optimum requires the *simultaneous* fulfillment of *all* conditions. If even one is unattainable (which is always!) the others, though possibly still attainable, are not any more desirable. As the "theory of the second best" shows, to reach a "second best" optimum the nonfulfillment of one condition requires the nonfulfillment of all.

---

[2] For detail, consult Robert H. Haveman and Kenyon A. Knopf, *The Market System* in this series, pp. 152–167.

[3] See R. G. Lipsey and K. Lancaster, "The General Theory of the Second Best," *Review of Economic Studies*, 1, 11 ff. (1956).

It is definitely not true that the more marginal conditions are fulfilled the closer we get to an optimum. In fact, we might make things worse. There is no a priori way of telling which of several states of the economy, each of which is characterized by the fulfillment of some and the nonfulfillment of other marginal conditions, is the better one. In short, unless the government could bring about at the same time the fulfillment of all marginal conditions, which short of magic it cannot, there is no way of telling whether its actions on behalf of efficiency increase economic welfare or reduce it.

III. INEQUITIES IN INCOME DISTRIBUTION

The *income distribution* in the real-life capitalist economies of today is typically not regarded as desirable either, though there is no "scientific" answer on that issue, as we have seen. Many people detect within themselves a strong sense of injustice as "luxuries" of the rich take precedence over the "needs" of the poor. Short of government intervention, there is nothing to prevent the superior purchasing power of the rich from exerting a stronger impact on the direction of resource use than does the pittance of the poor. The whims of the rich for yachts and swimming pools, for exotic foods and even psychiatrists for their pets, are satisfied long before the poor get adequately fed, clothed, housed, educated, and provided with medical care. Even in the United States only a few years ago, that fifth of all families with the lowest incomes received only 5% of total income, the richest fifth received 43% of the total. The inequality in wealth —that is, the things people own, rather than their annual income— is even more pronounced. This explains to a large extent the high incomes received by the rich, which are frequently incomes from the ownership of capital and land rather than labor. Even their labor income is frequently relatively high, since the wealthy find it easier to get specialized training. However, not all of this must necessarily be for the bad. To the extent that the rich, rather than leading what some might consider idle and repulsive lives, give their lives to public service or encourage research and the arts or invest large savings in new capital increasing the productivity and real income of other inputs, they do in fact perform a useful service for society. Still, many would agree that the *degree* of inequality of income and wealth should be less. Progressive income taxes taking a larger *percentage* from higher incomes, subsidies to the poor for housing and education, and inheritance taxes are examples of the attempt by modern governments to accommodate this general attitude.

IV. INSUFFICIENT GROWTH

Just as in the previous discussions of income distribution, it is not possible to give "correct" answers to the question of how well actual capitalist economies perform in the realm of *economic growth*. Certainly the endeavor of private firms to survive and make profits will in many instances help technical progress and will channel resources into the production of new capital goods, thus acting as an engine for growth. It can even be argued that imperfectly competitive firms, just because they are large relative to their markets, might be better able to finance such undertakings than the small firm of the competitive ideal. Yet again, innovation might be restrained by a securely entrenched monopoly eager to maintain the value of its present capital stock and to protect itself from the inroads of the new. So far as promoting growth by the production of more capital goods is concerned, this involves in a fully employed economy the reduction of output for consumption, and it has often been argued that households systematically undervalue future as opposed to present consumption. Notoriously unreliable in judging their own future, they prefer one bird in the hand to two in the bush. Therefore, *voluntary* restriction of consumption, releasing resources for investment in capital goods, might be considered inadequate. The modern monopolistic corporation might thus be a desirable device of forcing saving upon households by (a) withholding profits from owners as "retained earnings" and (b) competing for resources against consumers with such profits and new money created by the banking system. As a result, a smaller part of income earned gets into the hands of households to be spent on consumer goods and thus ties up resources in their production; or households spend all their incomes, but find that inflation caused by the insertion of bank credit into the stream of demand has eroded their purchasing power.

Be that as it may, many governments do consider the "automatic" rate of economic growth to be insufficient, as is especially obvious in the underdeveloped world. They therefore implement many policies to promote faster growth. Short of direct government investment, increased taxation of households to cut the demand for consumer-goods production coupled with easy credit for firms desiring to build capital goods might be a means of shifting resources from one use to the other. Yet, especially in the underdeveloped world, this might not be possible without drastic social and political reforms.

V. ENTER THE SOCIALISTS

It is precisely at this point that the proponents of socialism present their argument. If in all modern capitalist economies government seems to be needed to patch up an obviously imperfect system—to assure full employment, to implement efficiency, to correct the distribution of income, to promote growth—why not let the government "run the whole show"? It seems absurd, they argue, to allow private firms to operate when everything they do has to, in fact, be "corrected" by subsequent government intervention.

Even beyond that, if a perfectly competitive economy could ever exist and by society's standards did fulfill our four goals, government intervention would still be required! This would be so for at least three reasons.

A. Increasing Returns

First, for a certain initial range of output of any good, we are likely to meet a *principle of increasing returns*. The technically best way of producing a good might, for example, involve production in a plant of a certain minimum size full of assembly lines and automated equipment. Given such a plant, equal successive increases in some variable inputs, such as labor and materials, might bring about, not smaller and smaller, but larger and larger increases in output. As in Figure 5-1 between 0 and

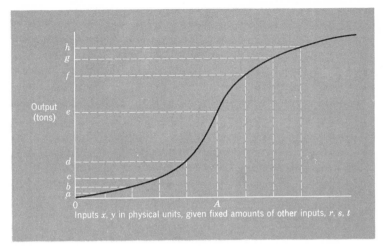

Figure 5-1.

A, we have an increasing marginal physical product. As we increase inputs *x* and *y* together (each "unit" being, for example, a combination of 1*x*, labor, and 7*y*, materials), given *r*, *s*, *t* (the plant and equipment), extra output rises from 0*a* to *ab* to *bc* to *cd* to *de*. The reason for this phenomenon is, of course, that there is some *technically* best combination of fixed inputs, *r*, *s*, *t*, with variable inputs *x*, *y*, which is *A* in Figure 5-1.

Until this combination is reached, output can be produced, but the fixed inputs are insufficiently utilized. As we approach *A*, their *technical* rate of utilization is ideal; for instance, there is one man per machine with just the right quantity of materials, as envisioned by the engineer. If we go beyond *A*, the fixed inputs become overworked; output might still grow for a while with increasing variable inputs, but at a much reduced rate. Here is our friend the principle of diminishing returns. (Note *de* > *ef* > *fg*, etc.)

All this, of course, could also be stated in a different way. Figure 5-2 is an exact duplicate of Figure 5-1. But now we ask how much additional variable inputs we need to increase output by successively *equal* amounts. The answer is as we should expect. As long as we have increasing returns of output to equal increases in inputs (from 0 to *A*), we need smaller and

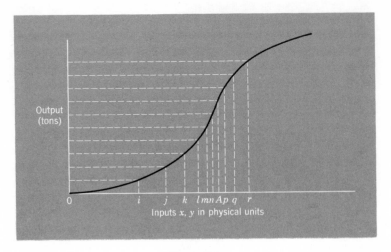

Figure 5-2.

smaller increases in inputs to get equal increases in output
($0i > ij > jk > kl > lm > mn > nA$). When we have diminishing returns of output to equal increases of inputs (after A), we
need larger and larger increases in inputs to achieve equal increases in output ($nA < Ap < pq < qr$). As output rises, marginal inputs are first falling, then rising. Evaluating the marginal
inputs (*hours* of labor and *pounds* of materials, for instance) at
their prices, we get marginal costs (*dollars* of labor plus materials). Hence marginal costs are falling and then rising with
increasing output, reflecting, respectively, the principles of first
increasing, then diminishing returns. This is illustrated in Figure
5-3, point A corresponding here to A in Figures 5-1 and 5-2.
Note that the firm's supply curve shown in Figure 4-2c is in fact
part of such a marginal cost curve to the right of point B. There
we showed that, given a price such as $0C$ in Figure 5-3, the
firm would maximize its profit (assuming that there is any) by
producing an output such as $0D$. But suppose output $0D$, not as
in Figure 4-2c, is so *large* relative to the market demand that our
firm producing there becomes one of very few firms in the industry. Then perfect competition breaks down, price $0C$ will not
any more be *given to* the firm, but can be *set by it*, and its

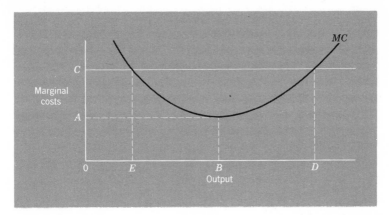

Figure 5-3.

profit will be maximized when price and marginal cost diverge, thus destroying the rationality of the price system.[4]

This, socialists argue, is very likely to happen. If perfect competition did exist, technical progress would quickly destroy it. Some firm at some time would be able, thanks to technical progress, to undersell all its competitors and still supply all or most of the market. Hence the government would have to intervene to rescue economic efficiency. But how? Shall it forbid technical progress? It certainly would not want to even if it could. Shall it allow technically modern plants to be built and then force them to produce such a small volume of output as to keep the market perfectly competitive? This would amount to asking firms to *minimize* their profits, as our firm would, for example, if it produced 0E where price also equals marginal costs. This also seems hard to do.

B. Need for Collective Consumption

↓Second, socialists would point out that certain goods in a perfectly competitive world, driven by private acquisitiveness, would never get produced because their production is not profitable. It may not "pay" any individual to purchase such *social*

---

[4] See Robert H. Haveman and Kenyon A. Knopf, *op. cit.*, pp. 159–160.

goods as battleships, court houses, schools, roads, hospitals, and parks, yet these and many other goods are needed for life in society. Even if some of these did get privately produced, their quantity would more likely than not be insufficient since everyone stands to gain from letting others buy such items first, and their collective purchase by government would have to be arranged.

C. Externalities

Finally, even a rational price system would have one major drawback, namely, failing to take account of *external repercussions of production and consumption.* As we have seen, the allocative virtue of the market mechanism assured under ideal circumstances equality of marginal cost and price ratios. However, the marginal costs involved were marginal *private* costs, that is, those incurred directly by the producer himself. It is quite possible and indeed likely, however, that private production involves costs to society at large which the particular producer does not pay and might not even be aware of. The generous amount of soot supplied by the smokestacks of a chemical plant, for instance, will raise the cleaning bills and imperil the physical health of people in the neighborhood; the noise and smells of the plant may frazzle the nerves of the abutters and raise their psychiatrist bills; the refuse dumped into the river may decrease the catch and raise the cost of fish hundreds of miles away, while the inhabitants of towns downstream may have to build new plants for purification of drinking water. The beauty of the countryside may be spoiled for all but the most insensitive brutes. Indeed, the whole character of a nation's life may be subtly changed by the collective efforts of private producers, as when we let round-the-clock television rob us of the ability to communicate with each other and to discover our own artistic talents. In short, marginal private costs of production may well understate the true costs to society, because they do not count the external effects of production which appear beyond the confines of the firm. In that case we shall be led in competitive equilibrium to produce too much of the good involved. Imagine two goods, *a* and *b*, being produced, with marginal private costs (MPC) equal to prices, so that

$$MPC_a = P_a = \$5 \quad \text{and} \quad MPC_b = P_b = \$10$$

Suppose further that the production of good a involves no external repercussions, but that of b one of $10; that is, the production of one more (or less) unit of b would, *in addition to* the producer's higher (or lower) cost of $10, involve costs to others of $10 more (or less). If consumers subjectively consider $2a$ worth as much as $1b$ at the margin, we have

$$\frac{MPC_a}{MPC_b} = \frac{\$5}{\$10} = \frac{P_a}{P_b} = \frac{MU_a}{MU_b} = \frac{1}{2}$$

Counting the marginal *social* cost (MSC) however, which is the MPC plus any repercussion on others, we have

$$\frac{MSC_a}{MSC_b} = \frac{\$5}{\$20} \neq \frac{\$5}{\$10} = \frac{P_a}{P_b} = \frac{MU_a}{MU_b} = \frac{1}{2}$$

In this case, consumers, guided by prices which *misrepresent* true relative social costs of production, are maximizing their well-being as far as they can see, as marginal utility and price ratios coincide. Yet it would be possible to increase society's welfare! By cutting production of b by one unit, $20, not $10, of resources are released ($10 in the factory, $10 elsewhere), and output of a can be raised by 4 units, since the extra cost of each a is $5. Consumers, valuing $2a$ as much as $1b$, are obviously better off for having received $4a$ for $1b$. Hence it would be desirable to force the producer of b to pay for the external cost, if it could be ascertained, by, for instance, a tax, making the price reflect marginal *social* cost. Then consumers would immediately buy more of a and less of b, until they valued subjectively $4a$ as much as $1b$:

$$\frac{MSC_a}{MSC_b} = \frac{\$5}{\$20} = \frac{P_a}{P_b} = \frac{MU_a}{MU_b} = \frac{1}{4}$$

Consumers would then buy b only in full awareness of what it really costs to society, they would buy it only to the extent that they felt their gain in welfare justified such costs.[5]

---

[5] In reality it would, of course, be next to impossible to ascertain the value of external costs and to impose the "correct" tax. Therefore, frequent use is made of more direct types of intervention, such as zoning laws, public health ordinances, etc.

Not all external repercussions of production are undesirable. Some firms, while engaging in their private activities, are conferring *benefits* upon others without being able to collect a revenue for this. (This, incidentally, is one reason for the need for collective consumption discussed in the previous section.) Think of an agricultural enterprise which afforests a certain region. Eventually this may favorably affect the climate with increased rain raising the yield, hence lowering the cost, of wheat production of nearby farms. Or imagine a pioneer firm coming into an undeveloped area. By building roads, laying telephone lines, or training the local labor force, it may make it considerably easier and cheaper for other firms to follow suit. Analogously with our previous discussion, such divergence of marginal private and social costs would call for encouragement of this activity, as by subsidies. Since the price equalling marginal private cost would now be *above* marginal social cost, consumers would be buying too little of this product.

The same type of external effects pervades the area of consumption. We have seen how the price system would bring into equality price ratios and marginal utility ratios. The latter referred, however, to marginal *private* utilities, that is, to the marginal satisfaction of the consumer himself. Private consumption may also affect others, as we know. The generous use of alcohol by some requires others to pay for extra police protection, not to mention the misery suffered by the families of alcoholics. The general habit of smoking forces society to forego some goods to free resources for cancer research and the building and maintenance of hospitals. The enjoyment of television by one drives his roommate to insanity; the good economic fortunes of one family causes another to be consumed with envy; and that new car on the road increases the inconvenience of everyone else, motorists, pedestrians, policemen, and town planners alike!

In short, marginal private utility may well exceed utility to society, because it does not count the effects on other persons. Though we might wish to ignore some of these effects (to hell with the envious, let them suffer!), we shall not feel this way in all cases. Hence we shall be led to consume too much of some goods unless we interfere with the rational price system. Imagine two goods, a and b, being consumed with the ratio of marginal private utilities (MPU) equal to that of prices and marginal costs, $P_a = \$5$ and $P_b = \$10$. Suppose, further, that the consumption of a involves no external repercussion, but that of b does: at the margin, the satisfaction of the consumer of b is half offset by the dissatisfaction with his consumption by those around him.

$$\frac{MC_a}{MC_b} = \frac{\$5}{\$10} = \frac{P_a}{P_b} = \frac{MPU_a}{MPU_b} = \frac{1}{2} \neq \frac{MSU_a}{MSU_b} = \frac{1}{1}$$

In this case, producers, guided by prices which *misrepresent* true relative social preferences, are producing goods in correct amounts as far as they can see, as marginal costs equal prices. Yet society's welfare can surely be increased. By cutting production of b by 1 unit, $10 in resources are released, enabling producers to produce 2 more a. *Society*, unlike the individual consumer, valuing $1a$ as much as $1b$, is clearly better off. By raising the price of b to the consumer through a tax (on alcohol or cigarettes or automobiles, for example), he is made to consume the good with undesirable repercussions more sparingly.[6] This will raise the MSU by raising MPU and reducing the negative external effect on the satisfaction of others.

External repercussions of consumption can also be beneficial. Neighbors enjoy beautiful gardens as well as the gardener, and a new telephone installed increases the satisfaction not only of him who pays for it, but also of his friends, who can now call him. Clearly then, it would be desirable to encourage and expand the consumption of those goods where the marginal social utility exceeds the marginal private one. Subsidies for medical care are a case in point.

We have said enough to show that ideally efficiency should assure that relative prices reflect relative marginal *social* costs and utilities.

$$\frac{MSU_a}{MSU_b} = \frac{P_a}{P_b} = \frac{MSC_a}{MSC_b}$$

---

[6] In reality, more direct types of intervention are also used often, such as speed limits and city ordinances against sale of alcoholic beverages to minors, against noise in apartment houses, etc.

Analogous arguments can, of course, be made for the factor market. Therefore, the larger the external repercussions, the smaller the faith we can place in the perfectly competitive model, even if it worked perfectly!

D. Summary

This then is, in a nutshell, the socialists' claim: perfectly competitive capitalism, that world guided by the "invisible hand," if it existed, would require constant government intervention. This would be needed, unless we are prepared to leave to chance whether or not the social interest is served. Government must keep the system from collapsing into imperfectly competitive markets on all fronts. It must correct for certain basic failures, such as inadequate provision of social goods and external repercussions of production and consumption.

Any real capitalist economy is in fact imperfectly competitive. Therefore, further intensive effort would be needed to assure as much efficiency as would be achieved in the ideal model. In addition, more likely than not, further action will have to assure full employment and a "desirable" distribution and growth rate of output. No government can hope to achieve this by partial and haphazard methods. What is needed is a basic change in the system, namely, the jump into socialism, giving to the government control of the means of production and full responsibility to use them for the good of society.

6

Socialism: The Competitive Solution

The Italian economist Enrico Barone, as early as 1908, had shown[1] the theoretical possibility of centralized direction of an economy by a socialist government to maximize economic welfare. He pointed to the possibility of expressing the millions of interactions among households and firms as a vast system of independent equations with an equal number of unknowns, as had been shown earlier by Walras (see our discussion in Chapter 4). Such equations, Barone showed, completely coincided, whether expressing the economic relationships of perfectly competitive capitalism or those of a socialist economy. The *formal* solution is independent of *who* owns the resources available and even *whose* preferences are being satisfied by their disposal. Barone, however, was the first to recognize the *impracticability* of a *centralized* solution of this kind. Even if one could centrally collect the necessary information on continually changing demand, technology, and resource availability and even if one were willing to employ an army of officials for this gigantic task, it would then be necessary to solve the equations on paper, not to mention the supervision of the execution of the economic plan so derived. Such a solution on paper would be a priori possible only, however, if one were willing to be bound by traditional technical coefficients. (Techni-

---

[1] See his article, "The Ministry of Production in the Collectivist State," reprinted in English in F. A. Hayek, ed., *Collectivist Economic Planning* (London: Routledge and Kegan Paul Ltd., 1963), Appendix A.

cal coefficients indicate the quantities of inputs needed for the production of a unit of output.) Such coefficients are, however, *economically* variable; that is, not every *technical* possibility of production is equally advantageous *economically*. (See, for instance, the above discussion of the fourth marginal condition.) Only large-scale experiment can determine the economically most advantageous technical coefficient, that is, the lowest cost combination of factors, but production at minimum cost is essential for efficiency to be realized. Experiments, in which is determined the lowest cost combination of inputs, involve, of course, the establishment of some firms which afterwards will have to be destroyed, and of others which can be maintained, copied, and enlarged. Therefore, there is no *a priori* solution of the equations of general equilibrium. Yet a solution by a Central Planning Board, willing to experiment, was—though costly—clearly conceivable.

I. A FAMOUS DEBATE

In 1920, shortly after the Soviet Revolution had begun the biggest socialist experiment to date, the debate on the possibility of rational direction of a socialist economy came to new life. Ludwig von Mises initiated a lively discussion on the subject by denying even such *logical* possibility.[2] There being no genuine markets for the means of production (capital and land), he argued, since they are collectively owned and used and never bought or sold, there can be no pricing them or their services. Hence, von Mises held, there can be no economizing, because of the absence of a rational price system, but only groping in the dark. Every departure from the private ownership of the means of production is, in fact, a step away from rational economics. "Socialism is the abolition of rational economy." Of course, von Mises did not deny that socialism was possible but he believed himself to have shown conclusively that *rational* socialism was a contradiction in terms, that a socialist economy must necessarily be less successful in the creation of welfare than a competitive capitalist one, that it must shatter on the rock of rationality.

---

[2] In his article, "Economic Calculation in the Socialist Commonwealth," reprinted in F. A. Hayek, ed., *op. cit.*, Chap. III.

Clearly, however, von Mises had gone too far. The *logical* possibility of a rational central direction of a socialist economy had already been shown by Barone. Prices of all inputs and outputs were part of the determinate solution of a system of equations, although such a solution was highly *impracticable.*

In 1938, Oskar Lange argued persuasively and brilliantly that this solution was not so impracticable after all. [3] He presented a blueprint of a socialist economy generally referred to since as "liberal or democratic socialism" or the "competitive solution." It can be summarized as follows:

II. THE MODEL

Suppose that socialism is established by one stroke in a democratic country, as for example, by majority vote of the population. Without any change in the *political* system at all, the *economic* changes required can be held to a minimum. In fact, we can envisage only four types of actors on the scene.

First, there are, as before, *households.* As before, they can *freely dispose of their own labor* in any way they desire unless they wish to remain voluntarily unemployed. Offering their services in free labor markets, they can enter any occupation for which they are qualified and receive as income whatever salary or wage is the going market rate. Unlike before, however, no household will have income from property, since all capital and land are now collectively owned. *Personal* income in the form of interest, rent, and profit will have disappeared.

On the other hand, households, as before, can also *freely dispose of their labor income*, buying with it any consumer goods they desire. They clearly cannot buy means of production, such as factories, coal mines, or agricultural land.

Second, there are, as before, *firms.* These producing units are now, however, collectively owned by all people. They are administered by *socialist enterprise managers,* who are salaried state employees, very much like the director of a modern capitalistic

---

[3] Lange's article has recently been reprinted in Oskar Lange and Fred M. Taylor, *On the Economic Theory of Socialism* (New York: McGraw-Hill, 1964).

corporation. As under capitalism, the enterprise managers use the capital and land at their disposal and buy labor services from households. They combine these inputs to produce outputs which they sell to households and firms. Enterprise managers are *given prices of inputs and outputs* and instructed to do two things: (a) to produce at lowest possible cost for any given volume of output (by combining factors as required by the fourth marginal condition, the minimum total and average cost for any conceivable level of output can be found), and (b) to select that volume of output where price equals rising marginal cost, that is, where profits are maximized or losses minimized. Following these two rules, the firms' demand for factors is determined.

Third, there is another group, *socialist industrial managers.* The manager of each industry is to regulate the number of firms in the industry so that the marginal cost *of the industry,* that is, the cost to the industry of producing another unit of output, whether with new or existing plants, is equal to price.

Finally, there is to be established a *Central Planning Board.* (CPB). It has the following three functions.

(a) It will determine the rate, but not the direction, of investment in the economy; that is, it will fix the percentage of all resources utilized in the production of new capital goods. This is to assure an "adequate" rate of economic growth and thus takes out of the hands of households the decision of how many potential consumer goods they are willing to sacrifice for their future betterment, or what the time-shape of the output flow is to be.

Elected officials are to realize the "correct" investment rate by setting a rate of interest such as to equate the supply of the services of capital goods with the demand. If the use of capital adds to output, the interest rate clearly cannot be zero, for then all firms would demand an infinite amount of capital to increase output and revenues at zero cost. But the social cost of capital goods produced and maintained is not zero; it involves the opportunity of consumption goods foregone. Since resources are scarce and consumption goods must be produced, the amount of capital goods that can be newly produced is limited. These, plus the existing capital stock, make up the supply of capital in any period. The demand has to be cut to this supply. Therefore, each firm has to pay to the government interest on the capital (and, incidentally, rent on the land) it uses, hence it cannot use capital unless it can recoup such costs in its revenues. A lower interest rate will, therefore, encourage, and a higher one discourage, the use of capital goods. The funds to acquire the capital goods used to begin with can, of course, be made available by the CPB, via industrial managers, to the firms out of tax revenue or the receipts from firms of interest, rent, and profits.

(b) It will determine the extent and kind of production of social goods to be consumed collectively, such as goods for defense and the administration of justice, education, health, etc. This may be financed, for instance, from the profits made by socialist enterprises, from their rent and interest payments, or from additional taxes on labor income. Hence consumers are collectively deciding through their government how much of all resources goes to make capital goods and collective consumption goods. Whatever is left goes to produce whatever kind and proportion of consumer goods households desire. It also is possible that government revenues exceed spending on new capital and social consumption before taxes on labor are imposed. In that case, households can receive a Social Dividend for their share in the ownership of capital and land.

(c) It determines the prices of all inputs and outputs. These prices are adjusted by trial and error until demand equals supply in all goods and factor markets. Until changed by the CPB, prices have to be regarded by all buyers and sellers as constant. The CPB is imitating, in effect, the free market in an attempt to find the kind of equilibrium solution illustrated in Figures 4-2 and 4-3 above and the rational price system discussed in Chapter 4. By making centralized price decisions only and letting output be determined in decentralized fashion, the socialist government has harnessed that "miracle machine," the market, to its task and is relieved of the need of solving on paper "those millions of equations." These equations are "solved," as in capitalism, whenever a household, on the basis of given prices that *it alone* cannot influence, decides on the supply of labor and demand for goods so as to maximize its welfare. They are "solved" again, as in capitalism, whenever an enterprise manager, on the basis of given prices that *he* is not allowed to influence, decides on the best factor combination and output scale, thus determining the demand for inputs and the supply of goods so as to maximize profits. They are "solved," finally, as would happen in capitalism by the voluntary entry or exodus of firms, whenever industrial managers, on the basis of prices that *they must regard as constant*, decide to permit the expansion of old or promote the building of new plants or see to it that capacity gets contracted instead.

Professor von Mises, the great *advocatus diaboli* of the socialist cause, had forced socialists to construct a blueprint that showed the possibility of a socialist economy guided by an adequate and practicable system of economic accounting to the maximization of economic welfare. "A statue of Professor Mises," said Oskar Lange, "ought to occupy an honorable place in the great hall of the Ministry of Socialization or of the Central Planning Board of the socialist state." And, indeed, by clearly and distinctly having formulated a problem, von Mises had made a major contribution to science.

III. AN ILLUSTRATION

Let us illustrate the Lange proposal with the help of an example. Suppose that there are two consumer goods industries, A and B, with three existing or potential firms in each. Their average and marginal cost curves are given in Figure 6-1 for the short run; that is, keeping each firm's plant and equipment fixed, these curves show the *minimum cost* attainable for each level of output with the factor prices prevailing. The derivation of these curves, therefore, is assumed to have occurred in accordance with the first rule given to the managers of socialist firms. For simplicity of exposition, we shall further assume that both industries are *constant cost* industries. This means that the expansion of production by *all* old firms or the entry of new firms will not cause a sufficiently large rise in the demand for resources to raise the prices of the resources used by the industry. Therefore the expansion of output by the industry will not cause the cost curves of all firms to shift upward. This is usually an unrealistic assumption, and anyone wishing to assume an *increasing cost* industry, where cost curves do shift up as the industry expands, may do so. This will complicate the analysis, but shall not alter qualitatively the point we are about to make.

Suppose that the price of good A has been set by the CPB at the level Oa and, following the rules of the game, is assumed to be constant by all firms at that level regardless of a firm's actions. Firm A_1 will dutifully select the rate of output where marginal cost (MC) equals price (P), that is, at the level Ob. Given its average cost curve, its AC at this output level will be bc, hence a profit of cd per unit is being made. Firm A_2, perhaps working with equipment of inferior quality or with less fertile land, has a higher AC at each potential level of output. Equating MC and P, it will produce output $O'e$ and make neither profit nor loss. Firm A_3, finally, is assumed to have a still higher AC curve. It would, were it to follow the rule, have to produce output $O''f$ where $MC = P$, making a per unit loss of gh, since AC exceeds P by this amount at this level of output.

Firm A_3, however, would not be allowed to be built or, if existing already, to remain in the industry. The *industrial* manager would decide that the additional cost of expanding output beyond A_1 or A_2 production is not justified by the additional revenue obtainable. Let us suppose that A_3 is in fact only a potential firm and that the demand for the output of industry A at price Oa equals the industry supply of Ob plus $O'e$. In this case, the CPB has no occasion to alter the price and has established an equilibrium price as \$1 in Figure 4-2b, for example.

Turning to industry B, let us suppose there are three firms producing quantities Oj, $O'k$, and $O''l$, respectively, and that this total also equals the quantity demanded in the aggregate. Hence Oi is also an equilibrium price. Since there is nothing in this economy to prevent consumers from spending their incomes so as to equate marginal utility and price ratios, and since all firms adjust their output to make marginal costs equal to the same prices, a rational price system will be established in the goods market.

Now let us test the workings of the system by assuming consumers to change their tastes, shifting their purchases away from industry B towards A. In terms of our earlier Figure 4-2b, the demand in A shifts as from DD to $D'D'$, while in B an opposite shift to the left occurs. Though the CPB knows the shape of neither the aggregate demand nor the supply curves, the change in consumer tastes will nevertheless be known to it. Statistical reports from industry A will indicate that the quantity

Figure 6-1.

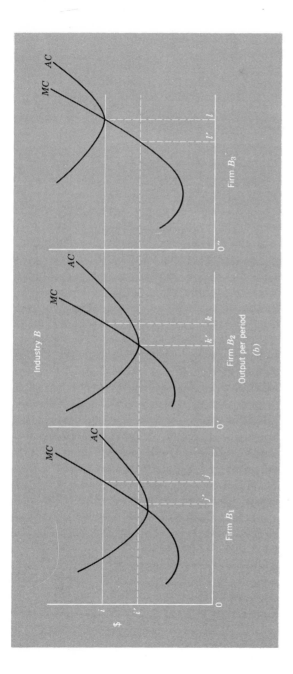

Figure 6-1 (*Continued*).

demanded at price $0a$ exceeds supply $0b$ plus $0'e$. Going back to Figure 4-2b, the CPB knows point E on the supply curve and is aware that E' on the obviously new demand curve is to the right of it. It will, therefore, following its own rule of behavior, *raise* the price of industry A's product. Similarly, it will lower the price of industry B's output, since reports will show that not all of quantity $0j$ plus $0'k$ plus $0''l$ is being sold.

Let the price of good A be raised to $0a'$, that of B lowered to $0i'$. Immediately, firm A_1 will increase production to $0b'$ where MC equals new P. Firm A_2 will raise output to $0'e'$ while, let us suppose, the industrial manager authorizes the construction of firm A_3 which will immediately produce $0''f'$. Profits of A_1 have clearly risen, in A_2 profits appear for the first time, and A_3 is producing with neither profit nor loss. Industry A's output has risen by a total of bb' plus ee' plus $0''f'$. Existing firms have increased output following the price signal and a new firm has entered. If by luck the new aggregate output now produced by three firms equals the quantity demanded at the new price, price will be maintained at level $0a'$.

Similarly, firm B_1 will cut output to $0j'$ (and its profits will fall), B_2 to $0'k'$ (and it will neither make profit nor loss). Firm B_3 should produce $0''l'$, where it would incur losses, but is shut down by the industrial manager. Industry B's output has fallen by a total of $j'j$ plus $k'k$ plus $0''l$. Existing firms have decreased output following the price signal, one has ceased to exist. If by luck the new aggregate output now produced by *two* firms equals the quantity demanded at the new price, price will remain at $0i'$. As it would be under perfectly competitive capitalism, demand has been accommodated. At the new equilibrium, though different from before, relative prices will again reflect relative marginal costs and utilities. In exactly analogous fashion, price adjustment by the CPB will continue until all factor markets are cleared, and a rational price system will also obtain there.

IV. THE CLAIMS

In fact, Oskar Lange asserts, the set of equilibrium prices will be reached *faster* than in perfectly competitive capitalism, as the CPB has an ideal overview of the whole economy and can take into account the probable effect of one price change on other markets. In any case, this economy would assure *efficient use of resources.* This would occur even if only one or two firms in an industry were needed to satisfy the demand. In capitalism, as we have seen when discussing the case of increasing returns, there would develop monopoly and inefficiency, because profits are then maximized if prices *exceed* marginal costs. Here, instead, all socialist managers regard price as constant *as a matter of rule* and equate *MC* to *P*. Further, Lange assures us, the socialist government would have no trouble judiciously taking account of external repercussions when setting prices (and it could be more *thorough* about it than a capitalist government) and it would not hesitate to demand all the goods needed for collective consumption. The extent of collective consumption would probably be much wider than under capitalism, as *democratic* socialism requires, for example, that all citizens, and not just the rich, get an equal opportunity of advancement by free education, free medical care, etc.

Since society also determines collectively the rate of investment, any desired *rate of growth* can be achieved, and this would not be left to accident. Furthermore, since resources diverted from the production of consumer goods would be immediately used to produce capital goods, there will be no reason that unemployment follow the act of saving. This, however, does occur in existing capitalist economies, where individuals' desires to save may be frustrated by incomes falling because no new investment is desired by firms, and hence resources are released into unemployment. *Full employment* in Lange's blueprint is assured by rapid adjustment of factor prices or government purchases.

Finally, we come to a matter closest to the hearts of many a socialist, *income distribution.* It would clearly be, Lange asserts, much more equalitarian, as no individual would receive income from anything but labor. To the extent that a social dividend would be paid from society's income in the form of profit, rent and interest, everyone would have an equal share. Labor incomes, however, would continue to differ, as they must, if one is to maintain proper incentives. But even then one may argue, since everyone has an equal *opportunity,* that those with higher labor incomes are simply getting rewarded for the sacrifice of working harder or longer or in unsafe occupations or of foregoing income to acquire skills. Taking into account such sacrifices, even labor incomes may be much more equal than appears at first glance. Obviously they will not be completely equal per "unit of sacrifice," since it is possible to be just the lucky owner of a skill that takes time to acquire and for which demand has suddenly and unexpectedly risen. Therefore, short-run differences in labor income can also reflect sheer *luck*. But efficiency requires such differences, for it is exactly the sustained wage differential that will eventually increase the supply of the particularly scarce skill. In general, however, it should not happen that some are starving while others indulge in luxury.

V. THE CRITICISM

In conclusion, it is only proper to remind ourselves that the blueprint of "competitive socialism" has never been tried out in reality and reality has a habit of differing from blueprints. Oskar Lange himself saw the greatest danger of his model in a *bureaucratization of economic life,* and others were quick to point out that even as "little" centralization of decision making as is envisaged by Lange might require a sizable tying up of resources in administration and in data gathering functions. It is also absurd to believe that the CPB and the hierarchy of managers, even if they could physically make all required decisions, would have all the knowledge or *initiative* required for this; although it may be easier to charge socialist than capitalist firms for external costs imposed by them on society, it would be just as hard to put a value on such external effects. Some decisions, regarding investment or large-scale research, for example, *cannot* be made on the basis of given prices but must be made on the basis of expected conditions. Hence the CPB must be *willing to approve of* risky change and, unless it is, its greater capacity to promote progress (compared even to large capitalist monopolies) may go unused.

Friedrich von Hayek has been particularly scornful of the alleged capability of the CPB to utilize the price system as an ingenious computing aid. Referring to the CPB's setting of all prices, he wrote:

This seems to be much the same thing as if it were suggested that a system of equations which was too complex to be solved by calculation within reasonable time and whose values were constantly changing could be effectively tackled by arbitrarily inserting tentative values and then trying about till the proper solution was found. Or . . . the difference between such a system of regimented prices and a system of prices determined by the market seems to be about the same as that between an attacking army where every unit and every man could only move by special command and by the exact distance ordered by headquarters and an army where every unit and every man can take advantage of every opportunity offered to them.[4]

He feels that the Lange scheme, when tried *in reality*, would be slower, not faster, in chasing after an ever-changing equilibrium in a dynamic world. It would be impracticable to change *all* prices frequently, as would be needed, hence they would be changed only after long intervals. Even then such price changes could not take account of millions of details requiring price differentiation with respect to quality and other circumstances of time and place.

Even worse, how is one to keep managers from cheating on the rules of the game? To put it differently, how is one to control and reward them?

There must be some criterion by which managers' salaries are set. Clearly he who "performs well" should be rewarded with better pay and promotion, and he who "does badly" should get dismissed or punished financially. It is an illusion to think that those responsible for decisions can be made to perform well if they do not have to pay for their mistakes and are not rewarded for their genius. Suppose profit were the criterion of performance. This might immediately give enterprise managers an incentive to cheat. As we have seen, all firms, even if they are one of two giants in an industry, are to act *as if* they could not influence prices. But in fact this is not so. Let us look as firm A_2 in Figure 6-1. It is originally producing $0'e$ at price $0a$, making neither

[4] Friedrich von Hayek, "Socialist Calculation: The Competitive 'Solution'," *Economica*, May 1940, pp. 130–131.

profit nor loss. Industry output equals aggregate demand. Suppose that the manager of A_2 were to cut output *contrary to the rule* to one half. If he was originally providing one third of the industry's output, this act would cut aggregate supply by about 17%. With demand unchanged, the CPB would discover a shortage and *raise the price*. Firm A_2 has, therefore, achieved exactly what its monopolistic capitalist counterpart would have done: it has raised price by cutting output. And at the higher price profits may well be made, thus giving a *personal* reward to the manager, although by having caused price to exceed marginal cost he has done what is socially undesirable, as our study of the marginal conditions has shown. Obviously, the CPB auditing apparatus cannot check all the records of all firms in detail to avoid this. If it did so, we would be back at full central decision making, which Barone has shown to be so utterly impracticable.

There could be a similar incentive to cheat for the *industrial* managers. Society's and their personal fortunes may well not coincide. They might wish to avoid investment, even if it seemed indicated under the rules. Their reward, if based on profit, depends *ex ante* on expected magnitudes but, since their prediction might go sour, *ex post* on how accurate they were at guessing. Obviously, investment will ultimately affect price by raising supply. But how? Hence they may simply avoid, because of personal reasons, the risk taking which is necessary for progress. Again, however, the CPB cannot possibly repeat all the calculations made by all managers to check on their loyalty. The CPB does not have, cannot have, and cannot use the divided knowledge which would be available to many entrepreneurs in perfectly competitive capitalism.

But, critics argue, it will be very tempted to become the omnipresent, omniscient holder of that knowledge. Hence Lange has indeed shown the Achilles heel of his model: the likelihood of extensive central direction and bureaucratization of economic life, hampering efficiency and progress alike. Even worse, some fear this will inevitably lead to a general restriction of personal freedom, as the government begins to use its enormous power to allocate resources for investment and collective consumption. At first, it will paternalistically try to change public opinion on these matters by propaganda, an organized campaign, very much like the advertising of private profit-making industry, to make people *like* future consumption and collective consumption rather than private consumption now. Eventually, however, there is bound to be, so the argument goes, authoritarian despotism. As propaganda fails to create the extensive agreement about society's goals that is desired by the government, it will impose those goals by force. A possible blueprint for such a socialist system is discussed in the following chapter.

7

Socialism: The Centralist Scheme I

Suppose that we were to topple the almighty consumer entirely from his throne. Not only shall he lose his private ownership of the means of production (capital and land), but also the right to choose his own occupation. Not only shall he lose the right to decide whether and to what extent resources are devoted to capital formation and collective consumption, but also his right to have the remaining resources allocated according to his passing fancy. Suppose that the CPB were transformed from a "mere price fixer," as some ardent socialists have sneeringly referred to that authority in Lange's "anemic socialism," into a *real* planner with complete authoritarian power over all matters economic. Like a doctor who prescribes a diet to his patients ("it's for their own good"), this CPB decides *centrally* and *in physical terms* how which inputs are used to produce what kinds and quantities of goods and who gets them. Once the CPB has drawn up a plan of economic activity over some future period, households and firms alike simply follow the instructions laid down for them. The *Plan*, not price, guides all economic life. In fact, the price system is now under suspicion of subtly sabotaging the construction of a socialist society. Reliance on it might give people what they want, hence build socialism on rotten foundations, if it is to take care of the problem that people don't know what is good for them!

I. THE USE OF INPUT-OUTPUT ANALYSIS

The first task that a central planning board would face under such circumstances would be the potential incompatibility of its decisions. Suppose it were to plan using all resources fully, and then proceeded to assign output targets for millions of goods. Possibly this would require more or fewer resources than are available. In the first case, the plan would be unworkable; in the second, it would not have achieved the goal of full employment. As we realize that the production of any one good, by requiring inputs, affects the production of many other goods, which in turn require the output of other goods as their inputs, and so forth *ad infinitum*, it becomes clear that the possibility of drawing up a plan which is internally inconsistent is all too great. A means must be found, therefore, to fence off the impossible, since efforts to achieve the impossible are bound to be a waste. This can theoretically be done with the help of input-output analysis, to which we now turn.[1]

A. The Transactions Table

This analysis revolves around the notion of economic interdependence referred to above, and one of its basic tools is the input-output table. Such a table shows how the *output* of each industry is distributed among other industries and sectors of the economy. Simultaneously, it shows the *inputs* to each industry from other industries or sectors. A hypothetical input-output or *transactions* table is given as Table 7-1. It has been enormously simplified for illustrative purposes by reducing from millions to a few the number of outputs and inputs considered. In reality, of course, a maximum amount of detail is desirable when constructing such a table. Table 7-1 gives us a short-hand description

---

[1] It must be pointed out, however, that input-output analysis can just as well be applied to economic relationships in a capitalist economy and could be highly useful in analyzing the structure of an economy, in forecasting likely changes, and in formulating government policies. It has in fact been developed largely in the United States under the leadership of Professor Wassily Leontief of Harvard. Nevertheless, though developed as an *analytical* tool, it can clearly be used as a *planning* tool.

Table 7-1. Input-Output (Transactions) Table, 1965

| Producer of Input | | Processing Sector | | | Final Demand Sector | | | | Total Gross Output (8) |
		Electric Power Industry (1)	Steel Industry (2)	Milk Industry (3)	Households (4)	Capital Formation (5)	Government (6)	Net Export (7)	
Processing sector	(1) Electric power industry (billion kwh)	50	200	50	150	0	50	0	500
	(2) Steel industry (million tons)	0	500	0	0	200	0	300	1000
	(3) Milk industry (million gal.)	0	0	10	70	0	10	10	100
Primary inputs	(4) Labor force (million man-hours)	2	13	2	0	0	3	0	20

of economic activity for a given country over some past period and is easily interpreted. It will be assumed that no economic activity except what is seen in the table has occurred and that the electric power, steel, and milk produced and the labor services rendered were completely homogeneous. Each *row* (reading from left to right) shows the output delivered by each industry or sector listed on the left side of the table to each industry or sector listed at the top of the table. Hence each *column* (reading from top to bottom) shows the inputs received by each industry or sector listed on top from the industries or sectors at the left.

The upper left corner of Table 7-1 has been set off by heavy lines and labeled *processing sector*. This part of the input-output table contains all the output of industries producing goods and services that was *produced and completely used up* within the processing sector during the period under consideration. There will be as many rows as columns in this portion of the table, and these would in a complete table include all types of agricultural outputs (milk being shown here), products of all manufacturing activities (electric power and steel being listed here), as well as construction, services of transportation, communications, whole-sale trade, etc. The remaining rows, read all the way across the table, show the disposition of the *services of primary inputs,* labor, capital, and land. This is represented in row 4 by labor only. Ideally, of course, there should be many rows, indicating the production, by differentiated groups in the labor force, of services of doctors, of steelworkers, of teachers, etc. Similarly, we can imagine placed here the services of a sector labeled capital stock. As we have seen earlier, the capital stock consists of all buildings and equipment and inventories in the economy. To the extent that these are used, this would be listed here. We can imagine, for example, the steel industry using hours of blast-furnace time (thus using as well as partially *using up* the capital stock, just as it used up newly produced electric power in row 1, column 2). Similarly, the electric power industry may utilize capital services by use of generating equipment or deple-tion of coal inventories produced and added to the capital stock in some past period (thus using up the capital stock, just as it used up newly produced electric power in row 1, column 1 or might use up newly produced coal to be listed in the processing sector). The services of land would be listed under primary inputs in the same fashion, distributing, for instance, acres used per year of each type of land.

Were one to turn the input data under any processing sector column into monetary units, one would recognize an old friend— the *cost* involved in any given productive activity. It would turn out, for instance, that the electric power industry had bought so many dollars worth of raw materials (electric power, coal, oil, etc.), listed as rows of the processing sector or intermediate inputs, plus so many dollars' worth of primary inputs, for which it incurred wages (for the use of labor), interest (for the *use* of capital), depreciation costs (for *using up* of capital), and rent (for the use of land). In our simplified example, only some raw material costs (electricity) and wages show up.

The remaining columns of the table, read all the way down, are labeled *final demand sector*. This represents the autonomous sector from which changes originate and are transmitted throughout the rest of the economy. Entries in the household column show receipts by households of goods and services for ultimate consumption. These can come from the processing sector in the form of electricity, or milk (listed here), television sets or clothing, bread or eggs, etc., or from the primary input sector, as the services of doctors, teachers, and domestics.

The column labeled capital formation needs special explanation. Here is listed the economy's new accumulation of new buildings, equipment and inventories, regardless of exactly who received them. Steel produced *and used up* would be listed within the processing sector, but steel produced and added to inventories, *regardless of by whom*, would be listed here. Similarly, buildings and machines produced during this year, unless completely used up in this year, would go under this heading (our column 5). This increase in the capital stock makes possible, of course, the future provision and use of more capital services than before, and this activity would then in turn show up in a row in the primary input sector.

The government column lists the receipts of all kinds of goods and services by governmental agencies (excluding in a socialist economy the receipt of capital goods by socialist firms, listed already in the processing sector or capital formation columns).

Analogous to the household column, government receives from the processing sector such items as electricity or milk (listed here), typewriters or army uniforms, jet airplanes, etc., or from the primary input sector services of administrators, judges, policemen (listed here), court houses, highways, and national parks.

Finally, the net export column shows the net receipt by foreigners of any of the goods or services mentioned so far. This exhausts total gross output, since it must either have been used up in the process of production (processing sector) or distributed among one of the final demanders listed. Though there are only these four types of final demand, each of them could again be broken down into any detail desired: households by size or even family name, capital by type, government by agency, and exports by country. As before, we can imagine the items in the final demand columns to be translated into monetary units. Then we would see that the sum of each column represented the total *expenditure* by the sector listed at the top. This would involve the consumption expenditure of households, C, plus the investment of new capital by firms, I, plus regular government spending, G, plus net exports, X. This would be nothing else but the gross national product.

Similarly, a translation of rows into monetary units would give us the total *receipts* of all industries from the sale of their output and the *incomes* of the owners of primary inputs. The sums of the primary input rows would give us the gross national income, a figure equivalent to the gross national product.

We shall, however, restrict ourselves to the physical input-output table. Row 1 tells us that of 500 billion kwh of electric power produced in 1965, 50 were used up in the electric power industry itself, 200 in steel making, and 50 more in the milk industry. Households consumed 150 billion kwh also, and government agencies 50 more. No electricity was added to inventories and if exports have occurred at all, they were exactly balanced by imports. Row 2 tells us that of 1 billion tons of steel produced in 1965, 500 million tons were used up in the steel industry itself, 200 added to inventories throughout the economy, and 300 exported net. No steel at all was delivered to the electric power or milk industries, to households, or to the government. Of 100 million gallons of milk produced by the milk industry, 10 were delivered to the processing sector, 70 million gallons to households, 10 to the government (as for the army), and 10 were exported (row 3). Finally, according to row 4, 20 million man-hours of labor were performed in 1965, 2 in the electric power industry, 13 in the steel industry, 2 in the milk industry, and 3 for government. No labor services were rendered to households or net to foreigners and, since it is impossible, no labor was accumulated in inventories.

B. Direct Technical Coefficients

Supposing that an input-output table like Table 7-1 has been constructed by the central planning board of a socialist economy in the greatest of detail for a past year, this table can become the basis of economic planning. Let us suppose that the detail is such that each "producer" listed on the left-hand side of the table is providing a homogeneous good or service. Let us further suppose that technically each output can be produced only in the one way implied by the table. Inputs cannot be substituted for each other and output can be raised by 10%, for example, only by increasing all inputs by 10%. The technical relationships implied by Table 7-1 can be summarized, as in Table 7-2, by calculation of *direct technical coefficients*, calculated for the processing sector only.

A technical coefficient shows the amount of inputs required from each industry on the left of the table to produce one unit of gross output of the industry listed at the top. Given our assumptions, since 50 billion kwh of electric power were needed to produce 500 billion, 0.1 billion kwh is needed to produce 1 billion kwh. Since no steel or milk were needed to produce 500 billion kwh, none are needed to produce 1 billion kwh. And since 2 million man-hours were needed to produce 500 billion kwh, 0.004 million are needed to produce 1 billion kwh. The other technical coefficients have an analogous meaning.

Table 7-2 shows the "first-round" effects of a change in the gross output of one industry on the industries from which it receives inputs. Any increase in steel production, by one million tons for instance, would require among other things an additional 13,000 man-hours of labor in that industry. But there will be

Table 7-2. Direct Technical Coefficients

Supplier of Output Input / Receiver of Output Input	Electric Power Industry (Per Billion kwh) (1)	Steel Industry (Per Million Tons) (2)	Milk Industry (Per Million Gallons) (3)
(1) Electric power (billion kwh)	$\frac{50}{500} = 0.1$	$\frac{200}{1000} = 0.2$	$\frac{50}{100} = 0.5$
(2) Steel (million tons)	$\frac{0}{500} = 0$	$\frac{500}{1000} = 0.5$	$\frac{0}{100} = 0$
(3) Milk (million gallons)	$\frac{0}{500} = 0$	$\frac{0}{1000} = 0$	$\frac{10}{100} = 0.1$

Appendix to Table 7-2: Labor Input Coefficients

(4) Labor services (million man-hours)	$\frac{2}{500} = 0.004$	$\frac{13}{1000} = 0.013$	$\frac{2}{100} = 0.02$

other repercussions, for additional power is also needed (0.2 billion kwh) which in turn can only be produced if additional labor goes into the power industry also. Hence an extra million tons of steel *cannot* be produced if available labor inputs have risen by only 13,000 man hours. The secondary, tertiary, etc. effects, which spread throughout the economy, will have to be taken into account, whenever an economic plan is being worked out.

C. Planning by Iteration

The aims of such a plan can now be expressed very simply by the Central Planning Board's establishing output targets by making entries *in the final demand columns*. The Board is clearly uninterested in the figures in the processing sector, as long as no more of any output is used up than technically necessary. On the other hand, the CPB's main concern is exactly to determine the types and quantities of goods made available during a year to households for private consumption, to government for collective consumption, to foreigners (as in the form of foreign aid), and for capital formation. Let us suppose our CPB, in considering the economic activity for 1966, wishes to leave all targets unchanged, except an increase of steel stockpiling from 200 to 300 million tons per year (row 2, column 5, Table 7-1). From what has been said above, we know that this cannot be accomplished by raising total gross steel output to 1,100 (row 2, column 8, Table 7-1). As column 2, Table 7-2, clearly shows, each million tons of steel produced requires a number of other inputs which require others in turn. How can the Central Planning Board draw up a consistent and feasible plan? The answer is that it will have to construct a table showing the direct *and* indirect effects of changes in final demand. Such a table would show the required total expansion of output in all industries as the result of a unit more output delivered to final demand. There are various methods for doing this, one being a step-by-step (or iterative) method. As we can see from Table 7-2, an increased steel delivery of even 1 million tons to final demands, requiring 1 million tons higher gross steel output, also requires 0.5 million tons more steel (row 2, column 2) to be used up within the steel industry. Hence gross steel output must rise by at least 0.5 million tons more, which requires an additional 0.25 million tons as inputs, and so forth. All this adds to $1 + 0.5 + 0.25 + 0.125 + \ldots$, equalling 2; that is, gross steel output must rise by at least 2 million tons, if 1 million more are to be delivered to final demand. Is this the end of the story? Two million tons of additional steel require, as Table 7-2 tells us, 0.4 billion more kwh of electric power (row 1, column 2), and if electric power production in turn required steel as input, steel output would have to be raised further. In our simplified case, this is fortunately not so (row 2, column 1). Similarly, neither steel nor power production require milk as input. Hence an increase of 2 (or 200) million tons of gross output of steel will enable us to deliver 1 (or 100) million tons to inventories, as desired.

Because of the simplicity of our example, we can now immediately set up a consistent plan for 1966, as is done in Table 7-3. The final demand columns are filled in arbitrarily after the CPB has made its political decision on this matter, as indicated above. As we have just shown, this implies that the entry in row 2, column 8 will have to rise by 200, that is, to 1,200. Hence we can fill in column 2, Table 7-3, in accordance with the technical coefficients of column 2, Table 7-2.

Since no milk is ever delivered to the electric power industry and final demand for milk is unchanged, row 3 of Table 7-3, as well as therefore column 3 of Table 7-3 will be identical to Table 7-1.

According to row 1, column 1 of Table 7-2, $\frac{1}{10}$ of electric power gross output will have to be delivered to the power industry itself, implying that $\frac{9}{10}$ are delivered elsewhere. Delivery to other processing sectors plus final demand is established as 490 billion kwh, which must be $\frac{9}{10}$ of gross output, giving us a gross output in row 1, column 8 of 544.44 billion kwh. Again using column 1, Table 7-2, we can fill in column 1, Table 7-3. Summing the entries in row 4, we get total labor requirements in column 8. Since we assumed technical coefficients constant, derivation of the technical coefficients from Table 7-3 would give us a table identical with Table 7-2.

Table 7-3 represents a *consistent* plan for 1966. Note how vividly the complete interdependence of the economy is demon-

Table 7-3. Input-Output (Transactions) Table, 1966 Plan

Producer of Input \ User of Output	Processing Sector			Final Demand Sector				Total Gross Output (8)
	Electric Power Industry (1)	Steel Industry (2)	Milk Industry (3)	Households (4)	Capital Formation (5)	Government (6)	Net Export (7)	
Processing sector								
(1) Electric power industry (billion kwh)	54.444	240	50	150	0	50	0	544.444
(2) Steel industry (million tons)	0	600	0	0	300	0	300	1,200
(3) Milk industry (million gallons)	0	0	10	70	0	10	10	100
Primary inputs								
(4) Labor force (million man-hours)	2.178	15.6	2	0	0	3	0	22.778

strated. Although only one single change was made in final demands, almost every single nonzero quantity outside the final demand sector had to be changed to maintain consistency.

Now we must ask whether this plan is also feasible. The answer depends entirely on the availability of the primary inputs, labor, land, and capital. In our simplified economy, labor alone is relevant. Hence the plan for 1966 can be carried out if, and only if, the labor put into electric power production can be increased by 178,000 man-hours and that put into steel by 2.6 million man-hours. This will allow the production of just the additional power and steel needed in the processing industries to fulfill the CPB's goal of increasing steel inventories as desired. If such primary inputs are not available, the plan cannot possibly be carried out, no matter how internally consistent it is.

Assuming, as is theoretically possible, that a consistent and feasible plan of this type has been worked out on paper in any desired detail, it is theoretically even easier for an all-powerful Central Planning Board to turn it into reality. It would simply translate this blueprint of economic activity into the law of the land so far as 1966 economic activity is concerned. Firms in the electric power industry would be *ordered* to produce 544.444 billion kwh of power and to deliver it to users, as shown in row 1, Table 7-3. Firms in the steel industry would be *ordered* to produce 1.2 billion tons of steel and to deliver it to various users as indicated by row 2. The milk producers would be *ordered* to produce 100 million gallons and deliver them as shown by row 3. Households, in return for receiving the goods and services shown by column 4, would be *ordered* to work 22.778 million man-hours, distributed among various occupations as shown in row 4. As a result of such a system of commands from on high, the government's program of capital formation, foreign trade, and collective consumption (columns 5–7) would be assured. Clearly, there is nothing in theory to prevent the CPB from trying about on paper until it has set up a plan using all primary inputs fully, however "full employment" may be defined. In our example, if in fact 25 million man-hours of labor were available, some or all final demand targets could be raised until a new plan variant using exactly 25 million man-hours is worked out. *Full-employment* being assured, any desired program of capital formation, collective

consumption, or export which is consistent with at least providing a subsistence real income to households (column 4)
can be carried out. A government bent on the most rapid *growth*
possible could maximize any desirable entries in column 5 at
the expense of entries in the remaining final demand columns.
This would, of course, increase in the following period the capital
stock services under primary inputs (not shown in Table 7-3,
but corresponding to labor services), and hence make possible
increases in one or all of the final demand targets. A government
anxious to increase collective consumption, be it in the form of
schools, hospitals, or intercontinental missiles, can maximize the
entries in column 6 at the expense of the remaining final demand
columns. A government could similarly promote aid to other
countries by pushing exports, or it could instead keep investment,
collective consumption and exports to a minimum, raising private
consumption as high as possible (column 4). This output among
households, furthermore, could be distributed in any manner
desired, thus achieving an *equitable distribution of output,* however defined. All of these things can be done, but the iron law
of economics—scarcity—is all too apparent. Final demands cannot be satisfied without limit as long as primary inputs are available in limited amounts. Any increase in one target, given a fully
employed economy, requires a decrease in another. That choice
no one can avoid.

D. Practical Problems and the Use of Computers

Now the time has come to ask the question about the *practica-
bility* of such a centralized direction of economic life. It will be
obvious to anyone that the gathering of the information on the
activity of a past year, that is, the setting up of a "realistic" Table
7-1, is by itself a gigantic piece of work. Hence it would be
necessary in practice to confine oneself to perhaps a few thousand
products and inputs, which would damage the degree of consistency achieved. Even worse, if such limited information can be
assembled in one place, the working out of a plan (such as
Table 7-3) from direct technical coefficients (such as Table 7-2)
and desired final demands becomes extremely complicated
mathematically. Luckily, the step-by-step calculation by hand,
which we engaged in above, can be replaced by another tech-

nique using high-speed electronic computers. This technique involves taking the difference between an *identity matrix* and the *input coefficient matrix* (Table 7-2) and calculating from this an *inverse matrix*. This sounds terribly technical, but is not really very hard to explain. The reader anxious to go on with the main argument may easily omit the special passage that follows (pp. 95–99) and proceed to Table 7-4 on page 99.

A Digression: Matrix Inversion. First, we have to define the meaning of the term matrix, which is any *rectangular array of numbers*. We may symbolize a matrix by $[a_{ij}]$, where i refers to the rows and j to the columns of the matrix. The technical coefficients of Table 7-2 (excluding its Appendix) could, for instance, be written in matrix form as follows:

$$[a_{ij}] = \begin{bmatrix} a_{11} & a_{12} & a_{13} \\ a_{21} & a_{22} & a_{23} \\ a_{31} & a_{32} & a_{33} \end{bmatrix} = A$$

The individual elements of this matrix refer in symbolic form to the entries in Table 7-2. Element a_{11} refers to the entry in row 1, column 1, or 0.1, while a_{22} refers to the entry in row 2, column 2, or 0.5. Sometimes it is convenient to simplify the notation even more and to represent a matrix such as $[a_{ij}]$ by a single capital letter like A.

Our matrix happens to be a square one, and the main diagonal of a square matrix is defined as all elements running from the upper left to the lower right corner, that is, all elements with equal row and column subscripts (here a_{11}, a_{22}, and a_{33}). A matrix which consists of 1's along the main diagonal, all other elements being zero, is called an *indentity matrix*. We shall symbolize it by I.

One matrix can be subtracted from another only if both have identical numbers of rows and columns. *Subtraction* involves, as the example below shows, taking the difference of *corresponding* elements.

$$I - A = B$$

$$\begin{bmatrix} 1 & 0 & 0 \\ 0 & 1 & 0 \\ 0 & 0 & 1 \end{bmatrix} - \begin{bmatrix} 0.1 & 0.2 & 0.5 \\ 0 & 0.5 & 0 \\ 0 & 0 & 0.1 \end{bmatrix} = \begin{bmatrix} 0.9 & -0.2 & -0.5 \\ 0 & 0.5 & 0 \\ 0 & 0 & 0.9 \end{bmatrix}$$

Matrix B, resulting from subtracting our direct technical coefficients matrix from an identity matrix, is, incidentally, called a Leontief matrix. It is this matrix that has to be inverted.

Matrix inversion is a most important step in input-output analysis. An inverse is that matrix which multiplied by the original matrix yields an indentity matrix. We shall label the inverse of any matrix B by B^{-1}. Let us suppose we wanted to find the inverse of our matrix B. Before we can do this, we have to introduce additional concepts, namely, those of a *determinant,* a *minor,* and a *cofactor.* At first sight, it is easy to confuse a determinant with a matrix, for a *determinant* is a *number of elements arranged in rows and columns to form a square,* such as

$$D = \begin{vmatrix} x_{11} & x_{12} \\ x_{21} & x_{22} \end{vmatrix}$$

As with matrices, the subscripts identify rows and columns.

A visual distinction used is that a determinant is enclosed in straight lines, a matrix in square brackets. A more basic distinction is, however, that a determinant *can be evaluated, yielding a single number.* The type of determinant illustrated above always is equal to

$$D = x_{11} \cdot x_{22} - x_{21} \cdot x_{12}$$

The above determinant, having two rows and two columns, is called a second-order determinant. The elements of a higher-order determinant can be expressed as minors and cofactors. Let us look at a third-order determinant, such as

$$D' = \begin{vmatrix} x_{11} & x_{12} & x_{13} \\ x_{21} & x_{22} & x_{23} \\ x_{31} & x_{32} & x_{33} \end{vmatrix}$$

The *minor* of any element of a third-order determinant consists of the second-order determinant remaining when the row and column of the element in question are deleted. Indicating minors by the symbol m, we can write the minor of x_{11} as

$$m_{11} = \begin{vmatrix} x_{22} & x_{23} \\ x_{32} & x_{33} \end{vmatrix}$$

Similarly, the minor of x_{23} would be

$$m_{23} = \begin{vmatrix} x_{11} & x_{12} \\ x_{31} & x_{32} \end{vmatrix}$$

The *cofactor* of an element, which we shall label C, equals the element's minor with an appropriate sign. If the sum of the subscripts of the element is *even*, as for x_{11}, the cofactor has a *plus* sign, if it is *odd*, as for x_{23}, a *minus* sign. Hence the cofactors of x_{11} and x_{23} are

$$C_{11} = + \begin{vmatrix} x_{22} & x_{23} \\ x_{32} & x_{33} \end{vmatrix} \quad \text{and} \quad C_{23} = - \begin{vmatrix} x_{11} & x_{12} \\ x_{31} & x_{32} \end{vmatrix}$$

Each of the cofactors can, of course, be evaluated as was determinant D, giving us

$$C_{11} = + (x_{22} \cdot x_{33} - x_{32} \cdot x_{23}) \quad \text{and} \quad C_{23} = - (x_{11} \cdot x_{32} - x_{31} \cdot x_{12})$$

A third-order determinant will obviously then have nine such cofactors. A third-order determinant is evaluated with the help of the minors of the first row, so that

$$D' = x_{11} \cdot m_{11} - x_{12} \cdot m_{12} + x_{13} \cdot m_{13}$$

Now we can return to the inversion of our matrix B. The steps involved are the following ones.

(1) Write the matrix as a determinant and evaluate it.

$$D = \begin{vmatrix} 0.9 & -0.2 & -0.5 \\ 0 & 0.5 & 0 \\ 0 & 0 & 0.9 \end{vmatrix} = 0.9 \begin{vmatrix} 0.5 & 0 \\ 0 & 0.9 \end{vmatrix}$$

$$- (-0.2) \begin{vmatrix} 0 & 0 \\ 0 & 0.9 \end{vmatrix} + (-0.5) \begin{vmatrix} 0 & 0.5 \\ 0 & 0 \end{vmatrix} =$$

$$0.9 \ (0.5 \times 0.9 - 0 \times 0) + 0.2 \ (0 \times 0.9 - 0 \times 0) -$$

$$0.5 \ (0 \times 0 - 0 \times 0.5) = 0.405$$

(2) Identify all cofactors of the determinant.

$$C_{11} = + \begin{vmatrix} 0.5 & 0 \\ 0 & 0.9 \end{vmatrix} = 0.45 \qquad C_{12} = - \begin{vmatrix} 0 & 0 \\ 0 & 0.9 \end{vmatrix}$$

$$= 0 \qquad C_{13} = + \begin{vmatrix} 0 & 0.5 \\ 0 & 0 \end{vmatrix} = 0$$

$$C_{21} = - \begin{vmatrix} -0.2 & -0.5 \\ 0 & 0.9 \end{vmatrix} = 0.18 \qquad C_{22} = + \begin{vmatrix} 0.9 & -0.5 \\ 0 & 0.9 \end{vmatrix}$$

$$= 0.81 \qquad C_{23} = - \begin{vmatrix} 0.9 & -0.2 \\ 0 & 0 \end{vmatrix} = 0$$

$$C_{31} = + \begin{vmatrix} -0.2 & -0.5 \\ 0.5 & 0 \end{vmatrix} = 0.25 \qquad C_{32} = - \begin{vmatrix} 0.9 & -0.5 \\ 0 & 0 \end{vmatrix}$$

$$= 0 \qquad C_{33} = + \begin{vmatrix} 0.9 & -0.2 \\ 0 & 0.5 \end{vmatrix} = 0.45$$

(3) Arrange the cofactors in matrix form.

$$\begin{bmatrix} 0.45 & 0 & 0 \\ 0.18 & 0.81 & 0 \\ 0.25 & 0 & 0.45 \end{bmatrix}$$

(4) Find the *adjoint matrix* which is the matrix of cofactors transposed, that is, interchanging rows and columns.

$$\begin{bmatrix} 0.45 & 0.18 & 0.25 \\ 0 & 0.81 & 0 \\ 0 & 0 & 0.45 \end{bmatrix}$$

(5) Divide each element in the adjoint matrix by the value of the determinant found in step 1. The result is the inverted matrix sought.

$$B^{-1} = \begin{bmatrix} 1.1111 & 0.4444 & 0.6173 \\ 0 & 2.0000 & 0 \\ 0 & 0 & 1.1111 \end{bmatrix}$$

(6) We can now check our result by multiplying our original matrix B by the inverse B^{-1}, which should give us an identity matrix I. Matrices can be multiplied only if they are *conformable,* that is, if the number of columns of the first equals the number of rows of the second. This is, of course, the case here with B and B^{-1}. The product will have as many rows as the first and as many columns as the second. The rule for multiplication can easily be derived from the detail that follows. It involves finding each element of the product matrix by cumulative multiplication of the elements of the first row of the first matrix by those of the first, second, etc. column of the second matrix, and so on.

$$B \cdot B^{-1} = I$$

$$\begin{bmatrix} 0.9 & -0.2 & -0.5 \\ 0 & 0.5 & 0 \\ 0 & 0 & 0.9 \end{bmatrix} \begin{bmatrix} 1.1111 & 0.4444 & 0.6173 \\ 0 & 2.0 & 0 \\ 0 & 0 & 1.1111 \end{bmatrix} =$$

$$\begin{bmatrix} \{0.9 \times 1.1111 + (-0.2) \times 0 + (-0.5) \times 0\} \\ \{0 \times 1.1111 + 0.5 \times 0 + 0 \times 0\} \\ \{0 \times 1.1111 + 0 \times 0 + 0.9 \times 0\} \end{bmatrix}$$

$$\{0.9 \times .4444 + (-0.2) \times 2.0 + (-0.5) \times 0\}$$
$$\{0 \times 0.4444 + 0.5 \times 2.0 + 0 \times 0\}$$
$$\{0 \times 0.4444 + 0 \times 2.0 + 0.9 \times 0\}$$

$$\begin{bmatrix} \{0.9 \times 0.6173 + (-0.2) \times 0 + (-0.5) \times 1.1111\} \\ \{0 \times 0.6173 + 0.5 \times 0 + 0 \times 1.1111\} \\ \{0 \times 0.6173 + 0 \times 0 + 0.9 \times 1.1111\} \end{bmatrix}$$

$$= \begin{bmatrix} 1 & 0 & 0 \\ 0 & 1 & 0 \\ 0 & 0 & 1 \end{bmatrix}$$

This proves our calculation of the inverse of B correct. B^{-1} is shown as Table 7-4.

Table 7-4. Inverted Leontief Matrix

Producer of Input	User of Output	Electric Power Industry (Per Billion kwh) (1)	Steel Industry (Per Million Tons) (2)	Milk Industry (Per Million Gallons) (3)
Electric power industry (billion kwh)		1.1111	0.4444	0.6173
Steel industry (million tons)		0	2.0000	0
Milk industry (million gal)		0	0	1.1111

Table 7-4 shows the required change in the gross output of the industries listed on the left if those at the top were to increase deliveries to final demand by the amount shown at the top. While Table 7-2 showed us that an increased delivery of 1 billion kwh to final demanders required immediately only 0.1 billion more of power within the processing sector, raising gross output to 1.1 billion kwh, we see here that counting the *indirect* effects also, we need to raise gross output by 1.1111 billion kwh. Steel and milk output, as in Table 7-2, would not be affected.

While in Table 7-2 we saw that an increased delivery of 1 million tons of steel to final demanders required immediately only 0.5 million tons of steel more within the processing sector, raising gross output by 1.5 million tons, we see here that counting the indirect effects, we need to raise gross output by 2 million tons. At the same time, while immediately only 0.2 billion extra kwh of power seemed required, in the end we will need 0.4444 billion kwh more. This is, of course, the exact result we obtained when deriving Table 7-3.

Finally, we learn from Table 7-4 that an additional delivery of 1 million gallons of milk to final demand requires an increase of gross milk output by 1.1111 million gallons and of power production by 0.6173 billion kwh. Leaving out all but the first-round effects, Table 7-2 would have suggested only figures of 1.1 and 0.5, respectively.

An inverted Leontief matrix thus becomes an indispensible planning tool for our Central Planning Board. With the help of such a table, it can immediately calculate all the consequences of any desired set of changes in final demands. Suppose it were to change final demands as drastically as shown in columns 4–7 of Table 7-5, given original Table 7-1. A new consistent table can be calculated rapidly with the help of Table 7-4:

(a) Deliveries of electric power (in billion kwh) were reduced to households by 100, but raised to government by 450, and to foreigners by 100, giving a net increase to final demand of 450. Hence, according to column 1, Table 7-4, gross power output must be raised by 1.1111 × 450 = 500, changing gross output to at least 1,000.

(b) Deliveries of steel (in million tons) were reduced to foreigners by 300, but raised to capital formation by 500 and to government by 100, yielding a net increase to final demand of 300. Hence, according to Table 7-4, column 2, electric power gross output must rise by another 0.4444 × 300 = 133.3333 billion kwh to at least 1,133⅓. Steel gross output must rise by 2.0 × 300 or 600 to at least 1,600.

(c) Deliveries of milk (in million gallons) were reduced to households by 60, but increased to capital formation (inventories), government, and foreigners by 90 each, yielding a net increase of deliveries to final demand of 210. According to column 3, Table 7-4, therefore, we have to raise electricity output further by 0.6173 × 210 = 129.633 billion kwh to a total of 1,262.9663. Steel output is not affected, but milk gross output must be raised by 1.1111 × 210 = 233.3333 to 333⅓. The results have been incorporated in the first three rows of column 8, Table 7-5.

(d) We can now use our technical coefficients of Table 7-2, assumed constant, to fill in columns 1–3. Adding across the first three rows, we get exactly the totals already calculated. The data

Table 7-5. Input-Output Table, 1967 Plan

User of Output / Producer of Input	Processing Sector			Final Demand Sector				Total Gross Output (8)
	Electric Power Industry (1)	Steel Industry (2)	Milk Industry (3)	Households (4)	Capital Formation (5)	Government (6)	Net Export (7)	
Processing sector								
(1) Electric power industry (billion kwh)	126.2966	320	166.6666	50	0	500	100	1,262.9663[a]
(2) Steel industry (million tons)	0	800	0	0	700	100	0	1,600
(3) Milk industry (million gal)	0	0	33.3333	10	90	100	100	333.3333
Primary inputs								
(4) Labor force (million man-hours)	5.0519	20.8	6.6666	0	0	100	100	232.5185

[a] Differs slightly from sum of row because of rounding.

in row 4 remind us that this plan is feasible only if the additional labor needed in the processing sector and needed in the final demand sector for government service or for work for foreigners is available. In this case, 212.5 million extra man-hours are needed, as a comparison of the sum of row 4 in Tables 7-1 and 7-5 shows. If 70,833 men entered the labor force working 10 hours a day for 300 days a year, this could be accomplished.

E. Criticism of the Model

We have already noted how enormous a task it would be to gather sufficient data to construct a fairly realistic transactions table like Table 7-1. Now we have shown that any use to be made of such information requires also the ample availability of fast and reliable computers to establish the inverse of the Leontief matrix and to calculate plan variants. On either count we can expect imperfections, if our model were to be put to the test of reality. Several other faults inherent in such a model, however, also deserve our attention. Having become absorbed in the question of consistency, we completely neglected *economic efficiency*. This has, indeed, been no accident, for there is nothing in this model of economic organization that would tend to bring about an economically efficient allocation of resources. If, as we have assumed for the time being, the input-output plan is couched entirely in physical terms and assigned by fiat to households and firms, there is no reason in the world to expect our marginal conditions, discussed in Chapter 2, to be fulfilled. The marginal utility ratios of consumers (conditions 1 and 7) will only by accident be equal to each other; that is, only by accident will he for whom a good is relatively more useful get assigned more of it until such ratios are equalized. The marginal cost ratios (condition 2) will only by accident be equal to each other, as firms are given physical output targets from the center which are sure to fulfill only one condition, namely, that all targets are technically consistent with each other. It is highly probable, however, that as firms receive such targets, as in the original situation in condition 2, that their MRT are *not* equal. The Central Planning Board has no way of knowing this, hence no way of reassigning output targets, as in the final position of condition 2, to increase output.

Similarly, the marginal physical products of any input in any production (condition 3) are likely to diverge among firms which are physically assigned quantities of inputs and outputs in the manner we have seen. The same, and for the same reasons, may hold for marginal physical product ratios (condition 4) among firms. All we know is that the assumption of fixed technical coefficients leads the Central Planning Board to double deliveries of all inputs to a firm which is to double its output. This, however, does not necessarily imply that all firms had identical quantities of all inputs and identical know-how to begin with. Hence there is amply room for diverging relative marginal physical products originally and after a change in the plan.

Our discussion implies already the likelihood of nonfulfillment of condition 5, which is a combination of conditions 1 and 2. Clearly, the same holds for condition 6. If people are *assigned* to jobs as well as being *assigned* real income, this condition most likely would not be fulfilled.

In short, although this type of planning may assure (not necessarily simultaneously) full employment, equity, or a desired growth rate, however one wishes to define these, it will do so at the expense of efficiency.

One aspect of this problem frequently receives special attention, namely, the assumed *constancy of technical coefficients* (Table 7-2) or the assumption of constant returns to scale. This assumption may be roughly correct for the very short run, but hardly over longer periods. Any long-term planning on this basis is certain to be marred by serious error. Technical coefficients are bound to change for at least three reasons.

First, if some *inputs can be substituted* for others, which is almost invariably true, it might be economically efficient to do so. In a market economy this would be done every time relative prices change (see our discussion of the fulfillment of marginal condition 4 in Chapter 4). Even if an economy had no monetary calculation at all, the same principle would apply. Suppose that the demands for labor and capital remain the same, but, because of population decline, the supply of labor falls. Labor has become relatively scarcer and should be economized more. (In a market economy the price of labor services would rise relative to capital services). Firms which are able should substitute capital for labor to assure economic efficiency. Insistence on production in accord with technical coefficients which are constant will lead to a lower total output than could be achieved. A similar example would be the gradual exhaustion of good coal deposits and the discovery of new oil fields. Unless (because of this increasing relative scarcity of coal relative to oil) the latter is substituted whenever possible for the former, output will be lower than it has to be. Scarce labor and capital will be wasted in the production of hard-to-get low-quality coal, while the same effort directed toward oil drilling and refining might provide the fuel user with a vastly greater input in terms of calories. While in a market economy a rising price of coal and falling price of oil would induce fuel users to make such a substitution, nothing of the sort would happen here, unless the Central Planning Board deliberately adjusted the technical coefficients in Table 7-2, slashing labor services and coal deliveries, but increasing the availability of capital services and oil.

Second, the growth of completely *new industries,* such as railroads, automobiles, aircraft, computers, or space rockets, may within a few years completely alter all input-output relations, requiring a thorough adjustment of all technical coefficients.

Third, even the *change of technical knowledge* within existing industries would require for its application the use of different technical coefficients in planning, which, unless reflected in prices that guide economic activity, will require a deliberate conscious action by the Central Planning Board.

One possibility for the CPB to effect such changes is the following. At any given time, some firms in any industry may be more advanced than others, using the latest equipment and most advanced techniques. If these can be identified, the CPB might use the input pattern of such "progressive" firms to plan the kind of input use it wishes to see in the economy as a whole. This assumes that the most advanced firms at any time are representative of the average of firms some time in the future. However, identifying the "progressive" firm is by no means an easy task. If labor is getting relatively scarcer, as in our example above, the "progressive" firm may be the one with the highest output per man-hour; but if labor is relatively abundant it may be economically wise to use it lavishly in place of capital and to have a *low* output to labor ratio. Further, we are implicitly assuming that there *are* some firms which have the ability and motivation for progress. If the economy is guided by the center in every detail, there may be no room at all at the level of the firm for such display of initiative! In any case, there is no escaping the need for judgment by the Central Planning Board. In the hypothetical economy we have sketched, *it* will have to decide how to change technical coefficients to reflect changes in relative scarcities of inputs or in technical knowledge. It may do so directly or by searching out and imitating the "progressive" firm.

8

Socialism: The Centralist Scheme II

In the previous chapter we have seen how input-output analysis might become a tool of central socialist planning, when it is desired to let a Central Planning Board decide in physical terms what gets produced and how. We saw that this method was hampered by the assumed fixity of technical coefficients. Is it possible, we ask now, to achieve the same ends without being so rigid, thereby improving efficiency? An affirmative answer is provided by the technique of *linear programming*.[1]

I. THE USE OF LINEAR PROGRAMMING

This is a technique for solving problems of optimization (maximization or minimization) confronting decision-makers who are subject to certain constraints limiting their actions on behalf of some goal. An example of such a *constraint* would be the availability of fixed quantities of certain inputs. A possible *goal* subject to optimization might be the value of output (to be maximized). As in input-output analysis, it is assumed that relations among data are linear: given any one production technique, for example, we find a proportional increase in all inputs yielding a

---

[1] This technique, like input-output analysis, is generally applicable to a great number of problems and not just the central planning of a socialist economy. It was developed in 1939 by Kantorovich in the USSR and later by Dantzig, Koopmans, and others in the United States, and it is a lineal descendant of input-output analysis.

proportional increase in output, that is, constant returns to scale. However, there might well be several alternative production techniques. Hence, unlike in input-output analysis, we allow for input substitution or variable technical coefficients. Having stated a linear programming problem, we proceed to solve it by a *systematic* trial-and-error procedure. Ordinarily the answer will not be found immediately, and in complicated problems it cannot be found rapidly without the help of electronic computers, but the solution is not arrived at by pure guesswork. Rather it follows certain rules, telling us unambiguously which step to take after we have taken the first one, and assuring us at the same time that each new step brings us closer to the desired optimum.

A. Single Production Technique

Let us introduce the method by temporarily holding on to the assumption of a *single* production technique subject to constant returns to scale. Table 8-1 summarizes our example.

Table 8-1. Linear Programming: Choice Among Final Uses

| | Production Activities | | Disposal Activities | | | | | |
| | | | Unemployment | | | Final Uses | | Constraints |
Activity	A^* (1)	B^* (2)	D_L^* (3)	D_K^* (4)	D_T^* (5)	D_A^* (6)	D_B^* (7)	C (8)
(1) A	−1	0.3	0	0	0	1	0	0
(2) B	0.1	−0.9	0	0	0	0	1	0
(3) L	2	3	1	0	0	0	0	180
(4) K	6	5	0	1	0	0	0	196.67
(5) T	1	3	0	0	1	0	0	90
Price	0	0	0	0	0	1.50	3.00	—

Goal: Maximize value of output delivered to final users.

The left-hand side of the table shows that there are five "activities" in the economy, the production of two commodities, A and B, and the use of the services of three resources, labor L, capital K, and land T, all five measured in some convenient physical units. The table is so arranged as to display how much "activity" is required from each type on the left to raise by one unit the level of activity listed at the top. *Outputs* are shown by *negative,* inputs by *positive* numbers, though the reverse would have been just as possible. Column 1 shows that the production of *one unit* of commodity *A*, called *A**, involves increased availability or output of 1*A* (hence −1 in row 1, column 1), and decreased availability or input of 0.1*B*, 2*L*, 6*K*, and 1*T* (hence the corresponding figures in rows 2–5, column 1). Column 2 tells us that 0.3*A*, 3*L*, 5*K*, and 3*T* are used as inputs per unit of *B*, called *B**, and (row 2, column 2) that the production of 1*B* raises the availability of *B* by only 0.9 units. This implies that 0.1*B* must be used up in the production of each *B* itself. Note that columns 1 and 2 contain the same kind of information as was contained in Table 7-2.

Columns 3–5 show the inputs required to bring about a unit of unemployment of *L*, *K*, or *T*, respectively. Obviously, only one unit of labor released from all other uses can increase unemployment of labor by one unit D_L*. Hence this column contains zeros in all cells except for row 3. Columns 4 and 5 have similar interpretations.

Columns 6 and 7 show the inputs required to bring about satisfaction of final demand with one unit of *A* or *B*, respectively. Obviously, only delivery of 1*A* can satisfy final demand for *A* with one unit D_A*. Hence only the first row contains the entry 1, all other rows zeros. Column 7 is analogously constructed.

Column 8 lists the constraints under which we must solve this problem. For the first two rows it tells us that whatever the *total* production of *A*, or *B*, its use in the processing sector for making *A* and *B* plus its delivery to final demand must exactly exhaust production, leaving zero of each good. For rows 3–5 it tells us that the *total* use of *L*, *K*, or *T* in production or in unemployment cannot exceed the totals available, which are 180, 196.67, and 90 units, respectively.

Now let us suppose a Central Planning Board, given the technical conditions and resource limitations of Table 8-1, has decided that it wants to maximize the *value* of total output delivered to final demand, having placed a price of 1.50 and 3.00 monetary units on a unit of *A* and *B*, respectively, if delivered to final demand. Similarly it attaches no value to *A* and *B* used up within the processing sector, nor does it attach positive or negative value to unemployment.

As an introduction to the solution of this problem, it is well to realize that Table 8-1 is simply a concise way of writing 5 equations (rows 1–5) with 7 unknowns (column headings 1–7). If we label the unknown levels of activities listed at the top of the table by a through g, we could write these equations as follows.

$$-1a + 0.3b + 0c + 0d + 0e + 1f + 0g = 0 \qquad (8\text{-}1)$$

$$0.1a - 0.9b + 0c + 0d + 0e + 0f + 1g = 0 \qquad (8\text{-}2)$$

$$2a + 3b + 1c + 0d + 0e + 0f + 0g = 180 \qquad (8\text{-}3)$$

$$6a + 5b + 0c + 1d + 0e + 0f + 0g = 196.67 \qquad (8\text{-}4)$$

$$1a + 3b + 0c + 0d + 1e + 0f + 0g = 90 \qquad (8\text{-}5)$$

A shorthand way of writing down the same information is

$$aA^* + bB^* + cD_L{}^* + dD_K{}^* + eD_T{}^* +$$
$$fD_A{}^* + gD_B{}^* = C \quad (8\text{-}6)$$

where all the capital letters are *column vectors*. A column vector is a special kind of matrix, consisting of any number of rows and a single column. (On the definition of a matrix, see above, p. 95.) For example

$$A^* = \begin{bmatrix} -1 \\ 0.1 \\ 2 \\ 6 \\ 1 \end{bmatrix} \quad \text{or} \quad D_L{}^* = \begin{bmatrix} 0 \\ 0 \\ 1 \\ 0 \\ 0 \end{bmatrix} \quad \text{or} \quad C = \begin{bmatrix} 0 \\ 0 \\ 180 \\ 196.67 \\ 90 \end{bmatrix}$$

A^* is, of course nothing else but column 1 of Table 8-1 and a way of defining a unit of activity A in terms of what it involves in other activities, here the output of $1A$, and the using up of $0.1B$, $2L$, $6K$, and $1T$. Since we are assuming linearity among all variables, we could also define three units of activity A as

$$3A^* = 3\begin{bmatrix} -1 \\ 0.1 \\ 2 \\ 6 \\ 1 \end{bmatrix} = \begin{bmatrix} 3 \times (-1) \\ 3 \times 0.1 \\ 3 \times 2 \\ 3 \times 6 \\ 3 \times 1 \end{bmatrix} = \begin{bmatrix} -3 \\ 0.3 \\ 6 \\ 18 \\ 3 \end{bmatrix}$$

which means that all effects will be tripled. In Equation (8-6), since we do not know how many units of A^* will be required to fulfill the program, the unknown a has been inserted instead of the 3.

Given our problem in the short-hand form of Equation (8-6), we can also state our goal in equation form:

$$\text{Maximize value } V = 1.50\,fD_A{}^* + 3.00\,gD_B{}^* \quad (8\text{-}7)$$

We now proceed with the solution according to the *Simplex Method*. It is based on two fundamental properties of linear programming problems. The first states that *the optimum solution to any linear programming problem will be a feasible basic solution.* Our system of 5 equations and 7 variables has a large number of solutions, and a *feasible basic solution* is any feasible solution to n equations having n activities (possibly some at a zero level). Having 5 equations, our "basis" should contain 5 activities and not violate the constraints; that is, it should be feasible. The other activities remain "outside the basis" with activity levels at zero. Since some of each commodity is required by any solution (see Table 8-1, row 2, column 1 and row 1, column 2), the production activity of each good must appear in any basis. A possible basic solution is

$$30A^* + 3.33B^* + 110D_L{}^* + 50D_T{}^* + 29D_A{}^* = C \quad (8\text{-}8)$$

This corresponds to Equation (8-6), leaving activities D_K and D_B outside the basis at zero; that is, there is neither unemployed capital nor delivery of B to final demand. Equation (8-8) could, of course, be split up into five equations as (8-1)–(8-5), or it can be written as

$$
30\begin{bmatrix} -1 \\ 0.1 \\ 2 \\ 6 \\ 1 \end{bmatrix}
+ 3.33\begin{bmatrix} 0.3 \\ -0.9 \\ 3 \\ 5 \\ 3 \end{bmatrix}
+ 110\begin{bmatrix} 0 \\ 0 \\ 1 \\ 0 \\ 0 \end{bmatrix}
$$

$$
+ 50\begin{bmatrix} 0 \\ 0 \\ 0 \\ 0 \\ 1 \end{bmatrix}
+ 29\begin{bmatrix} 1 \\ 0 \\ 0 \\ 0 \\ 0 \end{bmatrix}
= \begin{bmatrix} 0 \\ 0 \\ 180 \\ 196.67 \\ 90 \end{bmatrix} \quad (8\text{-}9)
$$

From this the five equations corresponding to (8-1)–(8-5) can be reconstructed, the first one reading

$$30 \times (-1) + 3.33 \times 0.3 + 110 \times 0 + 50 \times 0 + 29 \times 1 = 0$$

and stating that of 30 A produced, 30 were available for delivery outside A industry and were distributed as follows: $1A$ to B industry, 29 to final demand, none becoming unemployed labor or land (logical impossibilities).

According to Equation (8-7), the value of this solution is $1.50 \times 29 = 43.5$ monetary units.

The second feature of the simplex method now comes into use. It is a procedure for testing possible changes in the feasible basic solution, Equation (8-8). The *simplex criterion* states that an activity should be added to the basis (and an existing one deleted) if the net effect of this change is to improve upon the achievement of the goal, that is, in our case if it raises V. Once no activity outside the basis is more profitable than the equivalent combination of activities in the basis, the optimum is reached. We proceed to do this by expressing all 7 activities in terms of those contained in our basis.[2]

Column 1 of Table 8-2 lists the values of the 7 activities shown on the left side of the equality sign in the 7 equations, while column 2 lists the values of the equivalent combinations of activities presently in the basis and shown to the right of the equality sign. A comparison shows that substitution of $D_B{}^*$ into our basis for the equivalent combination of activities presently contained

---

[2] This involves nothing more difficult than solving 7 sets of 5 equations with 5 unknowns, 5 of which (rows 1, 2, 3, 5, and 6 in Table 8-2) are immediately obvious. Take row 4, Table 8-2, for example. It can formally be written as $D_K{}^* = vA^* + wB^* + xD_L{}^* + yD_T{}^* + zD_A{}^*$ which turns into

$$\begin{bmatrix} 0 \\ 0 \\ 0 \\ 1 \\ 0 \end{bmatrix} = v \begin{bmatrix} -1 \\ 0.1 \\ 2 \\ 6 \\ 1 \end{bmatrix} + w \begin{bmatrix} 0.3 \\ -0.9 \\ 3 \\ 5 \\ 3 \end{bmatrix} + x \begin{bmatrix} 0 \\ 0 \\ 1 \\ 0 \\ 0 \end{bmatrix} + y \begin{bmatrix} 0 \\ 0 \\ 0 \\ 0 \\ 1 \end{bmatrix} + z \begin{bmatrix} 1 \\ 0 \\ 0 \\ 0 \\ 0 \end{bmatrix}$$

or the 5 equations

$$0 = -1v + 0.3w + 1z$$
$$0 = 0.1v - 0.9w$$
$$0 = 2v + 3w + 1x$$
$$1 = 6v + 5w$$
$$0 = 1v + 3w + 1y$$

The solutions are given in row 4, Table 8-2.

Table 8-2. Simplex Criterion[a]

Equivalences [Basis Equation (8-8)]	Opportunity Value (1)	Present Value (2)	Possible Gain from Change (3) = (1) minus (2)
(1) $A^* = 1A^* + 0B^* + 0D_L^* + 0D_T^* + 0D_A^*$	0	0	0
(2) $B^* = 0A^* + 1B^* + 0D_L^* + 0D_T^* + 0D_A^*$	0	0	0
(3) $D_L^* = 0A^* + 0B^* + 1D_L^* + 0D_T^* + 0D_A^*$	0	0	0
(4) $D_K^* = 0.15A^* + 0.02B^* - 0.36D_L^* - 0.20D_T^* + 0.10D_A^*$	0	0.15	−0.15
(5) $D_T^* = 0A^* + 0B^* + 0D_L^* + 1D_T^* + 0D_A^*$	0	0	0
(6) $D_A^* = 0A^* + 0B^* + 0D_L^* + 0D_T^* + 1D_A^*$	1.50	1.50	0
(7) $D_B^* = 0.85A^* - 1.02B^* + 1.36D_L^* + 2.20D_T^* + 1.15D_A^*$	3.00	1.73	+1.27

[a] Calculations have been performed with many digits, although all results in this table are rounded.

in it would raise V. Introducing $\alpha D_B{}^*$ and deleting α units of its equivalent, we derive a new basis (coefficients rounded):

$$\alpha D_B{}^* - \alpha(0.85A^* - 1.02B^* + 1.36D_L{}^* + 2.20D_T{}^* + 1.15D_A{}^*)$$
$$+ 30A^* + 3.33B^* + 110D_L{}^* + 50D_T{}^* + 29D_A{}^* = C \quad (8\text{-}10)$$

$$\alpha D_B{}^* + (30 - 0.85\alpha)A^* + (3.33 + 1.02\alpha)B^* + (110$$
$$- 1.36\alpha)D_L{}^* + (50 - 2.20\alpha)D_T{}^* + (29 - 1.15\alpha)D_A{}^* = C$$
$$(8\text{-}11)$$

Since no coefficient in a basis can be negative (one cannot deliver negative products or leave resources unemployed which one does not have), α can at most be equal to 22.69, which would eliminate unemployment of land. Our new basis becomes (coefficients rounded):

$$10.77A^* + 26.41B^* + 79.23D_L{}^* + 2.85D_A{}^*$$
$$+ 22.69D_B{}^* = C \quad (8\text{-}12)$$

Its value is

$$V = 1.50(2.85) + 3.00(22.69) = 72.35 \quad (8\text{-}13)$$

This is an increase of 28.85, as should have been expected since 22.69 units of $D_B{}^*$, each adding net 1.27, were introduced.

In Table 8-3, we have once more checked on possible improvements of basis Equation (8-12). There is none, since any further change would leave V unchanged or lower it. Hence Equation 8-12 represents the best program under the circumstances:

(1) Production of 10.77 units of commodity A, of which $7.92(26.41 \times 0.3)$ should be delivered to B industry as input and 2.85 to final demand.

(2) Production of 26.41 units of commodity B, of which $1.08(10.77 \times 0.1)$ should be delivered as an input into A industry, $2.64(26.41 \times 0.1)$ as an input to B industry (note that entry -0.9 in row 2, column 2 of Table 8-1 is the sum of -1 denoting production and 0.1 denoting input use), and 22.69 to final demand.

(3) Of labor resources, $21.54(10.77 \times 2)$ go to A industry, $79.23(26.41 \times 3)$ to B industry, and another 79.23 remain unemployed, exhausting the total of 180.

Table 8-3. Simplex Criterion[a]

Equivalences [Basis Equation (8-12)]	Opportunity Value (1)	Present Value (2)	Possible Gain from Change (3) = (1) minus (2)
(1) $A^* = 1A^* + 0B^* + 0D_L^* + 0D_A^* + 0D_B^*$	0	0	0
(2) $B^* = 0A^* + 1B^* + 0D_L^* + 0D_A^* + 0D_B^*$	0	0	0
(3) $D_L^* = 0A^* + 0B^* + 1D_L^* + 0D_A^* + 0D_B^*$	0	0	0
(4) $D_K^* = 0.23A^* - 0.08B^* - 0.23D_L^* + 0.25D_A^* - 0.09D_B^*$	0	0.10	−0.10
(5) $D_T^* = -0.38A^* + 0.46B^* - 0.62D_L^* - 0.52D_A^* + 0.45D_B^*$	0	0.56	−0.56
(6) $D_A^* = 0A^* + 0B^* + 0D_L^* + 1D_A^* + 0D_B^*$	1.50	1.50	0
(7) $D_B^* = 0A^* + 0B^* + 0D_L^* + 0D_A^* + 1D_B^*$	3.00	3.00	0

[a] Coefficients rounded.

(4) Capital is fully used: 64.62(10.77 × 6) units in *A* industry and 132.05(26.41 × 5) in *B* industry.

(5) Land is also fully used: 10.77(10.77 × 1) units in *A* industry, 79.23(26.41 × 3) in *B* industry.

(6) Any attempt to change production, as, for instance, to eliminate labor unemployment, would *reduce* the value of final output which is 72.35 monetary units.

B. Several Production Techniques

The above was a sufficient introduction to linear programming to enable us now to go a step further away from the Leontief model and introduce the possibility of *alternative production technologies*. This is illustrated by expanding Table 8-1 into Table 8-4 so that there are two alternative ways of producing

Table 8-4. Linear Programming: Choice Among Technologies

		Production Activities					Disposal Activities			
		Industry A		Industry B			Unemployment		Final Uses	Constraints
Activity		$A_1{}^*$ (1)	$A_2{}^*$ (2)	$B_1{}^*$ (3)	$B_2{}^*$ (4)	$B_3{}^*$ (5)	$D_L{}^*$ (6)	$D_K{}^*$ (7)	$D_F{}^*$ (8)	C (9)
(1)	A	−1	−1	0.3	0.4	0.5	0	0	0.5	0
(2)	B	0.1	0	−0.9	−1	−0.95	0	0	0.5	0
(3)	L	2	3	3	6	4.5	1	0	0	80
(4)	K	6	7	5	1	3	0	1	0	110
Price		0	0	0	0	0	0	0	2.25	—

Goal: Maximize value of output delivered to final users.

commodity *A* and three for commodity *B*. However, to simplify calculations we assume that no land is used and that final output is required in fixed proportions (1*A* to 1*B*). Our objective remains the maximization of the value of final output ($\frac{1}{2}A$ plus $\frac{1}{2}B$ delivered to final demand being valued at 2.25 monetary units).

Assuming constant returns to scale and assuming that the effect of engaging in two activities simultaneously equals the sum of their separate effects (additivity), we can introduce the concept of a *derived activity*. Since a unit of *A*, produced by method A_1, requires as inputs 0.1*B*, 2*L*, and 6*K*, while making available 1*A* outside A industry, the assumption of constant returns to scale assures us that

$$0.5A_1{}^* = \begin{bmatrix} -0.5 \\ 0.05 \\ 1 \\ 3 \end{bmatrix}$$

Were we to produce $0.5A$ by technology A_1 and another $0.5A$ by technology A_2, it would involve

$$0.5A_1{}^* = \begin{bmatrix} -0.5 \\ 0.05 \\ 1 \\ 3 \end{bmatrix} \quad \text{and} \quad 0.5A_2{}^* = \begin{bmatrix} -0.5 \\ 0 \\ 1.5 \\ 3.5 \end{bmatrix}$$

On the assumption of additivity, $1A$ can, therefore, be produced by the derived activity A_1A_2, and

$$A_1{}^*A_2{}^* = \begin{bmatrix} -0.5 \\ 0.05 \\ 1 \\ 3 \end{bmatrix} + \begin{bmatrix} -0.5 \\ 0 \\ 1.5 \\ 3.5 \end{bmatrix} = \begin{bmatrix} -1 \\ 0.05 \\ 2.5 \\ 6.5 \end{bmatrix}$$

that is, by using $0.05B$, $2.5L$, and 6.5 K and producing half an A with each of the two technologies.

We can now proceed to exclude from further consideration all production methods that from a *technical* standpoint are inefficient. *Technological inefficiency* exists if there is a method or combination of methods capable of producing a given output with less use of one input and no greater use of others. In our case this is clearly B_3, for the derived activity B_1B_2 uses less of one input (A) and no more of the others than does B_3.

$$B_1{}^*B_2{}^* = \begin{bmatrix} 0.35 \\ -0.95 \\ 4.5 \\ 3 \end{bmatrix} \leqq B_3{}^* = \begin{bmatrix} 0.5 \\ -0.95 \\ 4.5 \\ 3 \end{bmatrix}$$

Inspection of Table 8-4 reveals that a basic solution must include both industries, A and B. Since we are left with 2 technically efficient methods in each industry, there are four types of basic solution, involving technologies A_1 and B_1, A_1 and B_2, A_2 and B_1, or A_2 and B_2.

We shall proceed by restating our problem so as to eliminate the first two rows of Table 8-4. We do this by finding the activity level of each of the four basic solutions mentioned, if final demand is at the level 1. Combination $A_1{}^*$ to produce A and $B_1{}^*$ to produce B gives the following equations (corresponding to rows 1 and 2 of Table 8-4):

$$-1x + 0.3y + 0.5z = 0 \qquad (8\text{-}14)$$

$$0.1x - 0.9y + 0.5z = 0 \qquad (8\text{-}15)$$

Since z (final demand) is held at 1, $x = 0.6897$ and $y = 0.6322$.

We can now form the following combined activity using x, y, and z as weights:

$$X_{11} = 0.6897A_1{}^* + 0.6322B_1{}^* + D_F{}^* = \begin{bmatrix} 0 \\ 0 \\ 3.276 \\ 7.2992 \end{bmatrix}$$

This means that producing 0.69A by method A_1 and 0.63B by method B_1 will use 3.3L and 7.3K while delivering 0.5A and 0.5B to final demand.

We can now make analogous computations for the remaining three combinations of technologies. All such combined activities will have zero coefficients in the first two equations enabling us to eliminate them and to replace Table 8-4 by its new version of Table 8-5, using only combined activities. We still have included

Table 8-5. Linear Programming: Table 8-4 Restated in Combined Activities

Activity	Production Activities				Disposal Activities		Constraints
	X_{11} (1)	X_{12} (2)	X_{21} (3)	X_{22} (4)	$D_L{}^*$ (5)	$D_K{}^*$ (6)	C (7)
(3) L	3.276	4.895	3.667	5.1	1	0	80
(4) K	7.299	4.947	7.444	5.4	0	1	110
Industry A: x	0.6897	0.7290	0.6667	0.7			
Industry B: y	0.6322	0.5729	0.5556	0.5			
Final Demand z	1	1	1	1			

all production possibilities (if *technically* efficient) from the original version.

Table 8-5 contains the labor and capital needed per unit of composite final output. If we wanted to know the required activity levels for 50 units of the (composite) final output, we would only have to multiply to coefficients of Table 8-5 by 50 and get the solution of Table 8-6.

Table 8-6. Linear Programming: Several Technologies, Final Output 50

Activity Levels	X_{11} (1)	X_{12} (2)	X_{21} (3)	X_{22} (4)
Industry A	34.49	36.45	33.34	35
Industry B	31.61	28.65	27.78	25
L	163.8	244.75	183.35	255
K	364.95	247.35	372.2	270

Column 1, Table 8-6 tells us, for instance, that producing $34.5A$ by method A_1 and $31.61B$ by method B_1, while using 163.8 units of labor and 365 units of capital, would enable us to deliver 50 composite units to final demand (in our case $25A$ and $25B$).

Now we can eliminate the remaining inefficient solutions. Our example is simple enough to lend itself to a graphical exposition. Table 8-5, containing the labor and capital inputs per unit of composite final output, can be used to construct the equal-product curves of Figure 8-1, each showing all combinations of labor and capital producing the same final output.

The labor-capital ratio used in activity X_{11} (combining A_1 and B_1) is shown by line OX_{11}, and similarly for the other activities. Points a, b, c, and d show the quantities of labor and capital needed to produce a final output of 15 by the various combined methods. We now see graphically what could also have been seen from Table 8-6, namely, that the same output produced with method X_{21}, rather than X_{11}, or X_{22}, rather than X_{12}, uses more of all inputs, and hence X_{21} and X_{22} are inefficient. We can now easily construct an equal-product line for a final output of 15 by connecting the points nearest the origin, here a and b. Because of our assumption of additivity made above, we can be sure that any combination of labor and capital on the straight line between

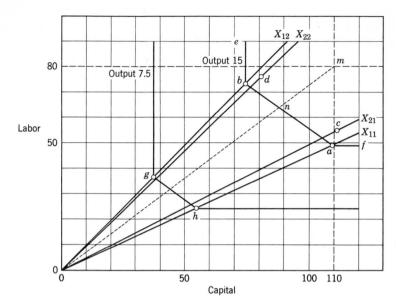

Figure 8-1.

a and *b* does also produce 15 units of output. The equal-product curve can be extended further by adding the disposal activities for labor and capital. This would extend the curve parallel to the axes from *b* towards *e* and from *a* towards *f*, respectively. Obviously, if 15 units of output can be produced with labor-capital combination *a*, they can also be produced with any combination along *af* using more capital and wasting it.

Since we also assume constant return to scale, we can halve all inputs and halve the output. Hence all other equal product curves can be constructed by scaling off proportional distances from the origin along rays $0X_{12}$ and $0X_{11}$. Half the distance $0b$ gives us *g*, half $0a$ gives *h*. Hence we derive the equal-product curve for an output of 7.5 units.

The optimum solution is now close at hand. The quantities of labor and capital available are plotted as the broken lines in Figure 8-1. Their intersection at *m* indicates the highest output attainable. Since it lies between the rays for efficient activities X_{11} and X_{12}, the solution will contain technologies A_1, B_1, and B_2.

The size of output can be estimated graphically as about 18.8 by considering the ratio $0m$ to $0n$. Algebraically we have only to solve our problem, as stated in Table 8-4, for $A_1{}^*$, $B_1{}^*$, $B_2{}^*$ and $D_F{}^*$ with the remaining activity levels at zero. This gives us

$$xA_1{}^* + yB_1{}^* + zB_2{}^* + qD_F{}^* = C$$

$$x\begin{bmatrix} -1 \\ 0.1 \\ 2 \\ 6 \end{bmatrix} + y\begin{bmatrix} 0.3 \\ -0.9 \\ 3 \\ 5 \end{bmatrix} + z\begin{bmatrix} 0.4 \\ -1 \\ 6 \\ 1 \end{bmatrix} + q\begin{bmatrix} 0.5 \\ 0.5 \\ 0 \\ 0 \end{bmatrix} = \begin{bmatrix} 0 \\ 0 \\ 80 \\ 110 \end{bmatrix}$$

The solution of this set of four equations is

$$\begin{aligned} x &= 13.39 \\ y &= 4.62 \\ z &= 6.56 \\ q &= 18.76 \end{aligned}$$

The optimum program can now be stated in plain English to require the following:

(1) Production of 13.39 units of commodity A by technology A_1. This would make available the same amount for delivery outside A industry, of which 4.01 units should go to B industry ($4.62 \times 0.3 = 1.386$ units to be used in technology B_1, $6.56 \times 0.4 = 2.624$ units in B_2) and 9.38 units to final demand (18.76×0.5).

(2) Production of 11.18 units of commodity B. $4.62B$ would be produced by technology B_1, requiring itself $0.462B$, hence leaving $4.158B$ for delivery elsewhere. $6.56B$ would be produced by technology B_2, all of which is available for delivery elsewhere. Of $10.718B$ free for delivery outside B industry, $1.339(13.39 \times 0.1)$ go as input to A industry, leaving 9.38 units for final demand.

(3) Of total labor resources, $26.78(13.39 \times 2)$ go to A industry (technology A_1), the rest to B industry, where $13.86(4.62 \times 3)$ units of labor will be used in technology B_1 and $39.36(6.56 \times 6)$ in technology B_2. There is no unemployment.

(4) Of total capital resources, $80.34(13.39 \times 6)$ go to make A by technology A_1, $23.10(4.62 \times 5)$ to make B by technology B_1, and $6.56(6.56 \times 1)$ to make B by technology B_2. This exactly exhausts capital resources available.

(5) Final demand receives $9.38A$ and $9.38B$ (18.76×0.5). This fulfills the requirement stipulated in advance that $1A$ be

delivered for 1*B*. It also maximizes the value of final output at 42.21 monetary units (18.76 × 2.25). Any different program would violate this goal, providing final output either in wrong proportions or of smaller value.

C. Shadow Prices

The reader who has followed the argument to this point will be able to realize how massive a task it would be to solve linear programming problems involving millions of goods each producible by a variety of methods. Yet it is also understandable how tempting it might be for a Central Planning Board to make use of this more realistic method. Indeed, this temptation may well be reinforced by the fact that any linear programming solution makes it possible to define *shadow prices* for all outputs and inputs. As a by-product of solving a linear programming problem, information emerges, such as the amount of output lost by the loss of one unit of a factor (the marginal physical product!) or the amount of one good producible by not producing a unit of another (the marginal opportunity cost!). *It would be possible to set relative monetary prices on the basis of such "shadow prices," so that the value of an input equals the value of its marginal physical product and the value of any output equals the value of that quantity of any other output which is producible with an equal amount of resources.* As Koopmans, for instance, has shown, such prices would be rational in exactly the same sense as the prices of the perfectly competitive economy under identical circumstances of demand and technology.[3]

Once proper relative prices for all outputs and primary factors have been established, the execution of the plan might well follow monetary incentives without direct central supervision. Firms making losses would indicate that they are misusing society's resources to produce something worth less than the opportunity of something else foregone (which is reflected in the cost of properly evaluated resources). By attempting to maximize profits, firms would in fact choose the correct technologies in producing whatever the Central Planning Board is demanding of

---

[3] See his excellent nonmathematical statement, "Efficient Allocation of Resources," *Econometrica*, October 1951, pp. 455 ff.

them. In principle, a Central Planning Board could continue to determine the composition of final demand (as our 1A for 1B). With the help of a gigantic battery of electronic computers, it could in theory determine the optimum program using all resources and the best combinations of technologies, while maximizing output produced in correct proportions. The incidental calculation of shadow prices, which are rational, would open vast possibilities for decentralized execution of the plan by employing such prices as levers to action. If we did not have to worry about the *practical* problem of data collection and calculation itself, we could hope to achieve, simultaneously, full employment, efficiency and any desired output distribution and growth within the limits of the possible.

9

The Soviet Economy

The time has come to turn to reality. A look at the Soviet economy, product of the oldest large-scale socialist experiment on earth, will serve that purpose. The Soviet Union is not a totally planned economy, as we have envisioned it in the two previous chapters, with every single transaction determined in advance. However, it certainly is a *centrally* planned economy of the general type discussed in Chapter 7.

I. GOALS AND STRATEGY

After the Revolution of 1917, there was no blueprint for the type of system the Soviets wanted to set up. Indeed, they were not even united on exactly what they did want. One is tempted to point to Marxism, their fanatically held sacred ideology, as a possible blueprint that might have been considered. But that was impossible, for the economic theory of Marx dealt with the future of capitalism and the forces making for its "inevitable" decline. Marxism could not be applied, as there was nothing in it about a centrally guided socialist economy. Hence the 1920's were years of discussion and experiment. The situation facing the new rulers was something like the following.

For more than two centuries, ever since Peter the Great, Russia had been experiencing the impact of modernization on its life. To be sure, the beginnings had been gradual and the pace of change had not picked up appreciably until after 1861, when the serfs were freed. Although power and property remained in the hands of a small, pleasure-loving aristocracy, more and more individuals had attempted and succeeded in the introduction of modern industrial techniques. From the 1880's to the First World War industrial output had been growing at 5% per year, and though the country was still backward in many ways, it seemed that it had reached its take-off for sustained growth. War and revolution, however, had caused great damage, possibly upsetting all hopes for continued economic progress. On the other hand, the revolution held great promise, too: the nation was in a frame of mind for things new, and huge reservoirs of ability had been brought to the surface, ready to be tapped. The Soviet leadership was determined not to miss this historic chance to leave backwardness behind forever and to catch up with and surpass the advanced capitalist nations in production. Indeed, as the years have passed, *rapid industrialization and economic growth* have become and remained *the basic obsession* of the USSR. In the 1920's, the question was *how* to achieve this objective.

In the wake of the revolution, large industry had been nationalized and land distributed among millions of peasants. After a period of general confusion, civil war, and popular unrest about the widespread use of brutal force (War Communism), Lenin had in 1921 instituted the *New Economic Policy* restoring capitalism in agriculture and trade, and making use of the market mechanism in guiding economic activity. Independent peasants were now allowed to sell any surplus product voluntarily in free markets, demanding and receiving industrial consumer goods in return.

The right wing of the Party, under the leadership of Bukharin, proposed an indefinite continuation of this policy after Lenin's death. Instead of wholesale requisitioning of agricultural output (as under War Communism) a limited tax in kind was to be imposed, the rest freely sold. Small-scale industry was to be denationalized and encouraged to produce goods wanted by the peasants. The expected increased supplies from the agricultural sector were to help turn the wheels of large-scale industry, supplying further goods to the countryside, and further stimulating production. Large-scale industrial output had increased more than threefold between 1920 and 1924, and such measures were believed to assure further cumulative growth. For a while, Bukharin's position against "monopolistic parasitism" of nationalized industry, that is, against the attempt to expand industrial capacity without increasing the standard of living of the (largely agricultural) population, was supported by Stalin.

But the Party's left wing, notably Trotsky and Preobrazhenskii, did not agree. They regarded Lenin's compromise with the demands of an individualist peasantry, even if unavoidable at the time, as a bitter defeat, which was to be reversed as quickly as possible. They pointed out the "success" of the New Economic Policy, increasing industrial output at record rates up to 1925, was by nature not sustainable. Large reserves of unutilized capacity and unemployed labor were being put to work, but the time was about to come when further growth of output would require increases in the capital stock in existence, as well as large-scale replacement of over-age equipment. Present "natural" rates of investment were insufficient for the task; hence it was up to the Soviet leaders to increase it. More of the industrial output had to consist of investment goods, less of consumer goods. To this, it was clear, peasants would react by producing, or at least delivering, less agricultural produce to the urban economy, crippling industry. *Force* was the only solution: a government monopoly of foreign trade had to insist on importing capital goods; prices *set by the government* were to be high for industrial consumer goods and low for agricultural output, reducing the real income of peasants to the barest minimum. Political tensions would mount, but eventually, after the capital stock (produced or imported with the resources released from consumption) had risen sufficiently, both investment and consumer-goods production could rise simultaneously. In the meantime, peasants had to be *forced* to produce as much as possible, and to give it up for as little as possible.

At the Fifteenth Party Congress, as Stalin consolidated his power, the left-wing "superindustrializers" were expelled, and many of them were exiled from European Russia in 1928. And maybe on the good old theory that some things are better done than said, Stalin proceeded in 1930 to institute in fact the draconic program of the Left! He acknowledged that "something like a tribute" had to be imposed upon the peasantry "in order to maintain and to develop further the present tempo of development of industry." [1] The device used was the collective farm. Large groups of farmers, rather than owning their land individually and being almost impossible to control, were compelled to pool it, own it collectively, and deliver large percentages of their output to the state at prices set by the state. [2] The management of such farms, officially elected by the members, but in fact appointed by, and loyal to, the state, made sure that peasants would "sell without purchasing." Officially, however, the collective farm was presented as a vehicle for the introduction of modern mass-production methods into agriculture. Rebellious peasants responded with a wholesale slaughter of livestock (in millions of heads, the numbers of cattle were 60.1 and 33.5, of hogs 22.0 and 9.9, of sheep and goats 107.0 and 37.3, of horses 32.1 and 17.3 in 1928 and 1933, respectively), while Stalin responded with the exile or extermination of 5 million peasants (kulaks). While coming to the point of explosion, the new device worked: agricultural output at first fell, industrial consumer goods became all but unavailable, *but the tribute was collected,* providing minimum food for industrial workers producing capital goods, and making possible exports to pay for record-breaking imports of equipment. The industrial workers themselves, controlled by trade unions loyal to Stalin, "consented" to work hard for future bliss. The Soviet Union was on her way, starving to glory. [3]

II. THE PLANNING MECHANISM

In the spring of 1929, the final draft of the first Five-Year Plan was approved, and was followed ever since by similar long-term development plans. Such plans, though far from perfect, have turned out to be a tolerable and acceptable tool of guiding the

---

[1] I. V. Stalin, *Sochineniia* (Moscow, 1949), XI, p. 159.

[2] In 1928, 400,000 peasant households out of 24.5 million were collectivized. By 1937, 18.5 million peasant households out of a total of 19.9 million were in 243,700 collective farms. Grain collected by the state was 12 million short tons in 1928, but 32 million in 1937, mostly from collectives.

[3] As someone put it recently, "while capitalism is an economic system based on the exploitation of man by man, in socialism it is the other way around.

economy along the path of growth. Ignoring finer details, the planning procedure can be described as follows.

During the first half of the year during which a plan is worked out (the planning year), the Central Planning Board (Gosplan) collects information on the state of the economy, showing accomplishments as well as any bottlenecks hindering further expansion. Though it is not set up in that form nor comprehensive enough, it is the kind of information that would be needed to construct a transaction table such as Table 7-1. Subsequently, the Presidium of the Party's Central Committee and the Council of Ministers study this information and determine the major objectives that are to be sought during the following year (the plan year). These might be cast in very general terms, such as "increase the share of resources devoted to investment by 10%" or "cease expanding the coal industry, and rapidly enlarge chemicals production with emphasis on plastics." In terms of our earlier discussion, this amounts to proposing changes in columns 4–7, Table 7-1. These *Party directives* are then used by Gosplan during the summer to work out a preliminary balance of the economy, specifying key output targets in physical terms as well as major inputs required for such outputs, as indicated by traditional technical coefficients. Here we meet the core of the plan, the system of *material balances,* showing for thousands of specified commodities (18,000 in 1963) the intended sources of supply and places of delivery. A typical material balance, greatly abbreviated here, might look like Table 9-1.

Table 9-1. Material Balance, 1966, Electric Power (Billion kwh)

Sources		Uses	
Production	544.44	Industry	
Imports	12.16	(a) Electric Power	54.44
Inventory decrease	—	(b) Steel	240.00
		(c) Milk	50.00
		Households	150.00
		Inventory increase	—
		Government	50.00
		Export	12.16
Total sources	556.60	Total uses	556.60

Listing in any desired detail all the sources and uses of a given commodity (material) and making sure that they are equal (balance), is simply a special way of writing down a *row* of an input-output table. Our Table 9-1 corresponds exactly to the information contained in row 1, Table 7-3. The fact that exports and imports balance was hidden in Table 7-3 above, since only *net* exports were reported. Setting up a *system of material balances,* as is done by Gosplan, corresponds, therefore, to setting up *an input-output table in disaggregated form.* However, this method does not exactly correspond to our blueprint described in Chapter 7 and was stumbled upon by accident. Since not all goods are included, it corresponds rather to the elaboration, probably by different people in different government offices and at different times, of *some* rows of the transactions table. Putting all material balances together and considering *all* goods produced would give us a table with innumerable gaps and inconsistencies. At this point in the planning process, furthermore, all entries are tentative.

The data just derived are called *control figures* and are passed down the administrative hierarchy during the early fall, for instance, to the various production ministries or regional planning centers. The Ministry of Electric Power might be told to produce 544.44 billion kwh in 1966, the Foreign Trade Ministry to import 12.16, and the steel industry to expect delivery of 240, for example.

As a next step, each ministry or regional agency in turn will split up the aggregate into subtotals. The Ministry of Electric Power might, for instance, allocate the production of 544.44 billion kwh among the Soviet Republics or other geographical units.

These in turn will add detail to the plan, passing it down to smaller geographic administrations and finally to the individual plants. Power plant X in the Ukraine will now have before it the control figures for 1966, telling it to produce 0.7 billion kwh, while expecting to receive x units of labor, y units of oil, z units of new equipment, etc.

At this point the process is reversed. Plant officials will suggest changes in the control figures, arguing possibly that the inputs provided could not possibly produce the output required and requesting an increase in input allocations. The *draft plan* is now passed back up the hierarchy until it reaches Gosplan again. At each level, the planning agency has to reconcile conflicting demands between the higher authority insisting on producing so much with so little and the lower ones arguing for producing less with so much more. At each level, an attempt is made to "tighten" the plan by shifting allocations among firms or regions and insisting that they do the job. If absolutely impossible, the imbalance is passed back up onto the higher authority. Eventually, Gosplan will have to resolve all remaining conflicts between sources and uses. Either targets have to be cut or more inputs must be made available.

The final balance being struck, the government approves the plan and turns it into *law*.

Now it is passed down the hierarchy of ministries, regional councils, etc. once more. At each step the plan law is again detailed until it reaches each individual firm. Firms are then required to enter with each other into legally binding contracts about the details of delivery to each other.

In addition to this physical core of the plan, concerned with high priority items, the production of goods and services considered less important is also planned, but in less detail and in *monetary* terms. Hence we have to consider prices. This is also necessary for another reason, namely, the fact that the execution of the physical plan itself is, among other ways, being supervised with the help of money flows, as observed by the State Bank.

III. THE ROLE OF PRICES AND MONEY

The Soviet government establishes essentially three types of prices and, once established, an attempt is made to keep them stable for as long a period as possible. The first type of prices is *wholesale prices for industry*. These are prices at which goods are sold from one firm to another. They are set to equal "planned, weighted-average, adjusted branch cost plus profit." It is here that for the first time we meet the real influence of Marxian ideology, for "cost" is interpreted in the Marxian sense, including only raw materials, depreciation, and labor, but excluding rent and interest. Before we proceed, a brief look at the Marxian position is necessary. Those familiar with it may wish to skip the special passage that follows (pp. 130–132).

A. A Digression: Marxian Ideology

At the center of Marxian economics is an explanation of exploitation based on the "labor theory of value." In an extremely simplified form, the argument can be paraphrased as follows:

Imagine that no single person went to work, neither in the factories, nor in the fields. Obviously, industrial and agricultural output would be nil. Hence *labor makes everything!* But does, in capitalism, labor get everything? Of course, not. Look ye, workers! Who made the factory you work in, but your employer owns? You did! Who made the car he drives, the clothes he wears, the champagne he brings home to his wife? You and your kind did! Yet he has all these things. Why? Because he defrauds and exploits you, because he takes interest and rent and profit, for which he does not work, and you get in wages what is left.

It is exactly this kind of argument, in this kind of language, that has aroused the irate feelings of many against the evils of an inequitable distribution of income and has made millions followers of Marx. When you are poor and others are rich, how comforting a thought it is to know that poverty can be explained, not because there is something wrong with you, but because you produce a lot, while someone else takes it away from you!

Of course, the trouble with this argument is that it can be turned upside down. Imagine that people went to work, finding neither factory nor soil. Would not output again be nil? Hence *capital and land make everything!* Capital and land should get everything, lest they be exploited by labor! This argument is not any more absurd than the first, and the truth of the matter is, as we have seen in Chapters 1 and 2, that all, labor, capital, and land, are productive. Just as I need my liver *and* my heart *and* most other parts of my body to live, though I would be dead without any *one* of them, I cannot argue that I live solely because of my heart. Capital or land, when added to labor, adds to output, just as does labor when added to them. They all are productive, they all are scarce, and they all must be priced for efficient use.

This does not mean, of course, that *private* owners of capital and land must get income from their utilization, as we have seen in Chapter 6. One can correct any undesirable income distribution due to private ownership of capital and land without denying the scarcity and productivity of capital and land. Such denial, unfortunately, was the effect of what Karl Marx did, though his presentation of the labor theory of value was somewhat more sophisticated than the above.

He argued that labor is the substance of all value and that the exchange value of everything was determined by the labor "socially necessary" for its production. If a laborer of average skill and intensity of effort were to use 5 hours to produce x pounds of coal and 10 hours to produce y pounds of iron ore demanded by someone (and if it were customary to produce these with one's bare hands), then the coal would be worth 5 hours of labor and the iron ore 10, and $2x$ coal should exchange for $1y$ ore. If another laborer were to spend 10 socially necessary hours turning the coal and ore into pig iron, the product would be worth 25 hours of labor. In Marxian terms, the value would be composed of "dead" labor, c (here materials used up), plus "live" labor, l (the human effort at the last stage of production). In a capitalist economy, however, labor would not receive all it produced, or l. If a man needed per day goods worth 2 hours to "reproduce himself in perpetuity" (such as feeding and housing himself, his wife, and their children who will replace them at death), his objective "worth" is 2 hours per day and so will be his wage, v. The capitalist will force him, however, to work longer, say $l = 10$ hours per day. If he used raw materials worth 3 hours and if he used up 1/1000 of a machine worth 1000 hours, dead labor of $c = 4$ was used and the value of the product was $c + l = 14$ hours. Marx would split l into wages v and surplus value s, writing the good's value as $c + v + s = 4 + 2 + 8 = 14$. Relative prices having been established in labor hours, they can, of course, be translated into any monetary units desired. In the real capitalist economy, according to Marx, since he has already identified c as raw materials plus depreciation costs, and v as wages, s corresponded to all forms of "exploitation": rents, interest, and profits. Such exploitation in capitalism, he argued, was not occasional or accidental, but ever present and unavoidable. It is not surprising, therefore, that many socialists have decried the charging of rent, interest, and profit and refuse to do so in a socialist economy ostensibly established to end exploitation. They would argue that the value of a good should equal dead labor c plus live labor l, with the s component being zero (unless it reflects the part of the product the laborer "shares" with society at large).

The definition of costs as $c + v$ is unfortunate from an allocative standpoint. Suppose that prices are set to be equal to average costs, and average inputs are as follows: Goods a and b both require 10 rubles of materials, 2 rubles of depreciation to replace used-up equipment, 10 rubles of wages, but in addition good a requires *use* of 1 acre of land and 10 times as much equipment as does b. According to Marxist reckoning, both goods would be valued alike at $c + l = 22$, where $c = 12$ and $l = 10$. Suppose a and b could be used equally well to produce *d*. Anyone using prices for allocation decisions would be indifferent about using *a* or *b*. Yet clearly use of *b* would be wiser, since the additional equipment tied up in *a*, as well as the additional land it requires, means that producing and using *a* involve a greater sacrifice of other goods foregone than do the production and use of *b* which would be indifferently chosen. Valuing goods at $c + l$ means treating capital and land *as free goods* available in unlimited quantities, which they are not. Hence a rent charge of, for example, 1 ruble per acre used per period, and an interest charge of, for example, 1% would remedy the situation. If the equipment used were valued at 1000 rubles for *a* and 100 rubles for *b*, we might value *a* at $22 + 1$ (rent) $+ 10$ (interest) $= 33$ (that is, $s = 11$) and *b* at $22 + 1$ (interest) $= 23$ (that is, $s = 1$). Hence those technically indifferent about using *a* or *b* would use *b*, minimizing the opportunity cost of other things foregone. Rent and interest do serve that function. Though one might not like private income of this type, one should not dismiss Marx's *s* as "mere exploitation of labor" which has no place in socialism. Even though part of *s* may at times represent exploitation, all of it does not. This was clearly recognized by Oskar Lange, who would continue interest and rent charges in his blueprint of socialism to preserve the allocative function of prices.

B. Industrial Wholesale Prices

Taking raw material, depreciation, and wage costs for all firms in a particular branch of industry, say tractor production, price setters would exclude from consideration abnormally high average costs of some plants as not "socially necessary." The remaining "adjusted" cost data are then weighted by the output levels of the various plants to find the adjusted branch average. Finally, this is changed (probably downwards) to a planned figure, taking into account expected cost declines due to technical progress, while a small percentage of such figures is added as profit, giving the price sought. Such profit is set for accounting purposes and ideologically defended as the workers' production "for society at large." It is obvious from what we have said that such industrial wholesale prices do in no way, except by sheer accident, reflect relative scarcities. This is so for a variety of reasons: the exclusion of rent and interest, the use of average rather than marginal costs, and the use of planned rather than actual costs.

C. Agricultural Prices

The second major type of price is *agricultural procurement prices* at which the production of farms has to be sold. These prices are set with the major objective of fixing the terms of trade of the peasants so as to allow them to receive no more consumer goods than desired by the state. Given the prices of inputs collective farms have to buy (mostly industrial wholesale prices) and the quantities they are supposed to buy according to plan (fertilizer, equipment, etc.), the price setters can estimate the revenue needed by the farms to cover their costs. If it were desired that collective farmers receive no money income whatsoever, since no industrial consumer goods are available for them, the projective cost figure would be divided by the planned output, establishing a delivery price per ton of product. If the output plan were fulfilled, the revenues would exactly cover costs, leaving no money income to the farmers. On the other hand, if it is desired that they have a negative (or positive) money income, because, let us say, farmers hold large idle money balances accumulated in the past (or there are industrial consumer goods available for them), the procurement price can accordingly be lower (or higher). Clearly, as in the case of industrial wholesale prices, prices so established would only by accident reflect relative scarcities of agricultural products. State farms, that is, those nationally owned, usually sell their products at the prices set for collectives, but workers in such farms have regular wage income, like those in industry.

D. Retail Prices and the Labor Market

A third major type of price is *retail prices* used by state retail stores (owned by the nation as a whole) and consumer cooperatives (owned, like the collective farms, by groups of individuals jointly). These prices differ in level and structure from industrial wholesale and agricultural procurement prices because of the imposition of a large and differentiated turnover tax on the latter two, providing a major source of revenue for the government. These prices are set with a view to clearing the aggregate market for each consumer good.

We have already seen how farmers may or may not have money income to demand goods offered in retail stores. Industrial workers are also paid in money for their work, though their income, as for laborers on state farms, is contractual and not residual like that of collective farmers. Workers have free occupational choice, and wages are differentiated by the state to get just the number of workers for each occupation that is required by the plan. This obviously minimizes the misery that would ensue if everyone were arbitrarily assigned to a job, as we envisioned in Chapters 7 and 8. If 200,000 coal miners are needed for the plan, that number will be procured, but, for example, by changing the wage up or down until that number is voluntarily forthcoming. Forced labor has shrunk to negligible proportions, but there are a few other qualifications to the above statement. The long-run supply of labor for various occupations is directed carefully by the state in controlling the number of people entering various types of training, and graduates are assigned to their first jobs. After a few years, however, they are free to do as they please, although the housing shortage seriously limits geographic mobility. Income earned by workers, as well as by farmers, can be freely spent; that is, there is free consumer *choice* and, unlike what we envisioned in Chapters 7 and 8, consumer goods produced are not assigned as income in kind. However, there is no consumer *sovereignty*. This means that the plan determines what kinds and quantities of consumer goods are produced, and each consumer decides which of these he wants. If any surplus or shortage for any one good should develop, production is *not* changed, as would happen if consumers were sovereign (see Chapter 6).

We can now return to the price-setting process. Planners make an estimate of consumer money income (wages, pensions, farm income) and deduct an estimate for other uses (taxes, saving). The result will be some figure such as 50 billion rubles. Planners also have (for instance, material-balance) data on planned availabilities of consumer goods (from production, imports, inventories minus exports, etc). These will consist of items such as 5 million tons of ham, 100,000 TV sets, 15 billion pounds of bread, 5 million rubles worth of kitchen utensils, etc. From these two types of information a set of prices is then derived so that the *value* of ham, plus the *value* of TV sets, plus the *value* of bread, plus the *value* of kitchen utensils, etc., equals 50 billion rubles. Then it is at least *possible* that consumers spend exactly what they had intended, while buying exactly what had been provided. On the other hand, many things can and usually do go wrong. There are obviously an infinite number of price sets fulfilling the above condition. If quantity demanded was at the set price different from the estimate (and such estimate *is* a wild guess, since there is practically no demand research), shortages and surpluses will occur. If the price of ham was set at 1 ruble per pound, demand may well be for 1 or 15 million tons, causing a surplus or shortage (and in the Soviet system, *no* change in production or price). Furthermore, output plans may not be (and for consumer goods usually are not) fulfilled. Hence shortages may occur, even if by accident the "correct" price set was picked, leaving undesired money balances in the hands of consumers.

Again, such prices obviously have no connection with relative scarcities. Identical prices for two goods will typically not indicate the use of identical quantities of resources in their production. Consumers may fulfill marginal condition 1, but condition 5, like 2, will be violated.

As a "safety valve" for things that might go wrong under the above conditions, the Soviets also allow one pure remnant of private enterprise, the *kolkhoz market*. In thousands of different locations, peasants are designated trading areas and allowed to sell freely agricultural produce grown on their private (about 1 acre per household) plots. Households can thus dispose of any excess money they might have and are unable to spend in retail stores. Prices in this market vary with supply and demand. The transactions, furthermore, serve the twofold purpose of providing extra, or even the only, money income to peasants and of allowing urban consumers to find an outlet for theirs. In both cases, this is an important element for incentives to work.

In summary, we can state that prices are essentially grafted onto the physical plan and manipulated to accomplish what has already been determined in that plan. That plan is usually expanded in monetary terms to include nonpriority goods, assigning to firms output and input targets in money, such as "produce 10,000 rubles worth of kitchen utensils, using 5,000 rubles worth of metal, 3,000 rubles worth of labor, etc."

E. State Bank Control

As a result of using money in the economy, it is possible to let the State Bank control the execution of the plan. Except for wage payments to households and their purchases of goods, the use of cash is severely restricted. Typically, an industrial or agricultural enterprise must deliver its output to other firms according to contractual obligations incurred as part of the detailed specification of the plan. Payment is not made by check, but by the acceptance method. The seller will send an order to pay to his State Bank office, which will deliver it to the buyer. Upon acceptance by the latter, the account of the buyer is reduced, and the seller's increased. In this way the State Bank can in theory check upon the purpose, timing, and size of every single transaction and prevent it unless it corresponds exactly to the predetermined plan. (Obviously, for the purpose of controlling real transactions via their counterpart money flows, any price set would do as well as any other. Hence the observed irrationality of prices is here irrelevant.) In fact, the State Bank has at its disposal stern sanctions, ranging from the expropriation of a firm's deposits to a full-scale Party investigation into enterprise affairs. Yet the burdens of surveying details of economic activity on the scale ideally required are enormous. Banks frequently only engage in "formalistic" controls, using sanctions sparingly and failing in their role of detailed overseer of the entire economy.

F. Incentives and Their Effects

Such detailed control missing, a number of things, having survived all administrative changes, go continuously wrong and have caused headaches for the central planners for many decades. The fact that a plan exists, no matter how feasible, internally consistent, and desirable it is, does not mean it will be carried out. Ultimately this depends on the *incentives* for work felt by millions of workers, peasants, and managers. We have already seen above that workers, whether in industry or on *state* farms, are essentially motivated by the same kind of rewards and punishments as in a capitalist economy. They receive wages and salaries with which they can buy goods in state stores or on the kolkhoz market. Their pay differs with the type of occupation they hold (training required, unpleasantness of work, importance attached to it by the planners) as well as the degree to which they exert themselves on the job (piece rates). Personal effort typically leads to promotion, lack of it to demotion or loss of job. In general, real incomes have risen steadily and substantially since the Second World War. All these things combined, there have been no particular problems with making people work. The case of peasants on collective farms is a different matter. Since they are, as we have seen, the ones from whom the "tribute" is collected, their incentives have been typically wanting, though much less so for work on their private plots! This, as well as the low priority given to investment in agriculture, must undoubtedly have contributed to the continued undesirable performance of agriculture in the Soviet Union. Agricultural output has grown substantially, but less so than hoped for by the planners.

The case of managers of industrial firms deserves some further study. Fundamentally, they, too, are motivated to do their best by the same kind of incentives as the managers of a modern capitalistic corporation, namely, salary and promotion. Yet the environment they work in is in many ways incredibly different. As we have seen, the Soviet industrial enterprise is given by some higher planning authority a plan, covering its operations for a certain period. This plan specifies a minimum output to be produced in value terms (and for priority goods in physical terms as well). It specifies input targets for materials, equipment, and labor in value and possibly physical terms. And it specifies a host of other goals, ranging from profits, quality, and labor productivity to winning socialist competitions and keeping the plants clean. A manager, as a steward for the state, is to do all these things and, upon performing well, will be rewarded with high pay as well as certain other things money alone may not be able to buy, such as a home, a car, and vacations at the Black Sea. On the other hand, failure to perform may bring not only loss of his job, but also prosecution for criminal negligence and (under Stalin) possibly a bullet in the neck.

To be more specific, while the basic salary may influence people to choose one occupation rather than another, it is a *system of bonuses* that determines what kind of decisions are made in the day-to-day operations of any one job. These decisions, as we shall see, are frequently made contrary to the interests of the state, although the bonus system is set up to encourage decisions desired by the central planners. Bonuses are received by management for fulfilling or overfulfilling the plan targets. It is quite possible to receive up to 50% of the basic salary for plan fulfillment alone and up to 4% more for each percentage point of overfulfillment. Hence the difference between 99 and 100% plan fulfillment may mean up to 50% difference in the incomes of the managing group, and a manager overfulfilling the plan by 5% may receive up to 70% above his basic money income! No wonder the system elicits high managerial effort.

The planning authority, however, in order to make the system work and judge managers, will have to provide the key to what is meant by plan fulfillment. This is a tricky problem, for it is possible to overfulfill three and underfulfill nine out of twelve different targets! The traditional response has been to give priority to the fulfillment of the *output* target in physical or, if not available, in value terms. This should not surprise us, since we have seen how central is the concern with physical planning of inputs and outputs.

We have now at hand everything needed to explain the behavior of managers. More than anything else affecting their bonus, output plan fulfillment will receive their undivided attention. This will begin with the elaboration of the plan itself. The lower the plan target, the easier it can be fulfilled. Hence the urge is strong to *hide the true capabilities of the plant.* But as we know, nothing is more vital to the central planner than to be informed of the capability of the economy as accurately as possible. Soviet planners are aware of this and have introduced the practice of "flushing out reserves" by arbitrarily increasing all production targets annually, even if they know of no capacity increase having occurred. This will, indeed, flush out some hidden capacities, but it will also make it impossible for other firms to fulfill an unfeasible plan, eliminating bonuses and incentives alike and possibly bringing criminal prosecution upon the innocent.

While excessively ambitious plans may raise the efforts of some managers to increase output (and also may raise their ulcer rate), they will also tempt managers to *over-order and hoard raw materials or labor.* This is another way of stacking the deck beforehand. By claiming that more material and labor are needed than is in fact the case, possibly more will be received. They can be used to overfulfill or they may "just be kept around" for insurance against future needs when materials might not arrive in time in right quantity and quality. Frequently personal influence (blat) is used with the higher authorities to have input allocations raised. As a result, all kinds of inputs may be available in all kinds of places but be unused, which is clearly not in the interests of the state. Many firms, especially those liable to insufficient deliveries of inputs since they produce low priority output, employ special kinds of supply expediters or "pushers" (tolkachi) who push, legally or otherwise, for the interests of the firm at higher places and who arrange for informal exchange of hoarded materials among firms. Hence hoards may be lower than one may think at first. However, the fact that materials probably go into *low* priority channels still shows this activity to be against the state's interests. Again, the state tries to counteract this activity by frequently moving managers from one job to another. This is to disrupt the "family relation," the system of mutual support of the controllers and the controlled, at the bottom of the planning hierarchy.

The *over-ordering of capital equipment* follows similar lines of reasoning on the part of managers. This is reinforced by the fact that fixed capital is provided as a grant. No interest payment being necessary, and no depreciation being incurred, if the equipment is not used, managers try to get as much as they can by whatever means. Possibly output can be increased, possibly unwanted equipment can be traded. In any case, there is nothing to lose and everything to gain. Even a steel mill can use a cabbage-planting machine!

The high mobility of managers, which is to counteract the above, provides them with an extremely short-range view. Hence they are unanimously *opposed to technical innovations. Replacing* present equipment with new capital is entirely different from getting more of the old. It is risky business, and risk is not rewarded. It will upset the apple cart by interrupting continuous production, and production *is* rewarded. To make things worse, at the very moment when a technical innovation is introduced, causing the need to eliminate production bugs, to retrain the labor force, etc., the output target is typically raised to account for the superior productivity of the new equipment or production method. At best this will mean no bonus, hence no wonder that managers drag their feet before introducing novelties! Nothing short of a direct order will do. Managers prefer to repair old equipment no matter what the cost, since their bonus depends on uninterrupted output. As a result, the introduction of new technology is seriously hampered. Planners have been quite at a loss to do anything about this reticence. Giving a special bonus for innovating will have no effect if it is small, and if it is large, the output goal will be ignored entirely.

Another serious problem for Gosplan lies in managers' response to the way in which the output target is stated, leading to the *production of low quality output and incorrect assortments.* To maximize output, managers are tempted to reduce quality. If the task is to produce tons of metal, greater impurity may not be visible, just as fewer stitches on a garment or fewer screws or thinner parts on a machine would not affect the number of garments or machines counted as output, freeing some inputs to raise output. At the expense of quality, this is hardly desirable. Again, if the choice is between 500 machines with or 550 machines without spare parts, we do not have to guess about the manager's choice, if his income depends on the number of machines produced. As a result, the Soviet Union has been plagued by persistent shortages of spare parts and complaints about low-quality output.

A related problem is the disregard of industrial and private consumers' demand. If small nails are needed, but the output plan is stated in tons, only huge nails will get produced. If the output plan is stated in numbers, only the tiniest ones will be made, and no large ones at all. This is the same if output targets are more general and stated in value terms, such as 50 million rubles worth of kitchen utensils. Only knives may be made, if that can most easily fulfill the plan, no matter what the demand for pots, pans, and can openers. If one were to specify the physical quantity and quality of each item produced, we would be back at the impractical case of overcentralization of bureaucracy.

In summary, we may say that Soviet managers, while following the plan as far as possible, do engage in a variety of practices contrary to the interests of the state when it becomes apparent that they cannot otherwise fulfill the plan. Being subject to a multitude of controls (the superior planning agency, the State Bank, the Central Statistical Administration, the Ministry of Finance, the Party, the Ministry of State Security), managers react in these ways rather than risk open falsification of fulfillment reports. But even in this way they continually place themselves in a potentially dangerous situation, since they do violate the laws. As one scholar put it, operating under tremendous pressure to perform, they are like a neurotic whose problems express themselves in psychosomatic illness. If one of these is cured, another one just as surely springs up. Somewhere, the pressure has to escape. It may make for a high ulcer rate, but it keeps the Soviet economy moving, and rapidly so.

IV. SOVIET ECONOMIC PERFORMANCE EVALUATED

In conclusion, how well has the Soviet economy done with regard to the four goals we have been discussing throughout this book? There is no doubt that it has not achieved efficiency, as we have abundantly shown. Prices being irrational, any decision made on their basis would be just as arbitrary as the many decisions made without regard to prices at all. Its income distribution, although only labor income exists, has been extremely unequal, rewarding managers of heavy industry or scientists out of all proportion to, say, collective farmers. But it has had full employment and spectacular economic growth. Although by no means all output targets were consistently fulfilled, those for priority goods typically were. This was made possible by the very nature of the rough material-balance-type planning which allows low-priority outputs to be sacrificed whenever the need arises to provide the inputs required by the core of the plan. Decisions regarded as adjustable get adjusted, that is, consumer-goods output. More than anything else, it was this ruthless determination of a totalitarian state to keep consumption from wolfing up output, to make possible capital formation, and to channel investment into those areas where the output to capital ratio was high that secured such unprecedented growth.[4] The wholesale copying of other nations' advanced technology, while building industries from the ground up and ignoring patent conventions, was an additional boon.

This is not to deny that big errors were made, nor is it to say that everything that did happen had to happen. Possibly much of the suffering of the population might have been avoided, while the same goal was achieved. Certainly some of the critical bottlenecks were broken with a crude brutality that might have done more damage than it repaired. Be that as it may, the strategy of Soviet development paid off and has now created an industrial colossus only second to that of the United States. Indeed, some western scholars have argued that the Soviet strategy of neglecting efficiency, while stressing investment and sheer output growth ("accumulate, accumulate—that is Moses and all the prophets"), might have been perfectly justified. They argue that commitment to economic efficiency might have wonderfully satisfied everybody's demand for toys, buttons, and cookies, but failed to do what was deemed necessary: tear asunder established ways of life and transform at breakneck speed a backward peasant country into a giant industrial-military power. Just as in the United States in wartime the economic priorities of the government were being enforced by quantitative direction, the USSR has continually achieved rapid results in priority sectors by having run, ever since 1928, what Oskar Lange has called, a "sui generis war economy." Although, at any given time, there might always be too few buttons and too many cookies, in the end there will be more of both than without growth. What of the future?

Any output growth can, of course, be used to boost growth further or to raise the standard of living. Since 1950, both have happened. It certainly is possible to continue devoting a large percentage of resources to investment, although the resultant output growth may be smaller, if investment for replacement

---

[4] Areas where the output to capital ratio is low, such as transportation, housing, municipal facilities, were neglected. The Soviets were lucky in having inherited much of this type of social overhead capital from the Czars.

grows in importance or investment in areas of low output-capital ratios is required. In addition, there is no reason to believe that the Soviets, having one day soon copied all there is to copy, cannot make technical progress on their own. The long-run view of their leaders speaks well for channeling resources into basic research, although the totalitarian setting may well at times, as in the case of Lysenko, stifle the spirit of free inquiry. But the Soviet educational system has in general been found to be excellent as to curricular content and level of achievement, and the facilities for basic research, directed toward no immediately useful discovery, have been found to be ample. There are, similarly, a great number of well-endowed institutes for applied research, which applies the results of basic research to practical problems. However, the centrally planned economy does have its defects in this area: research does not get started unless centrally planned, it does not get continued unless it has early success, it is unresponsive to demand and fails to make continuous improvements once "success" has been attained. This seems to be even worse on the level of the individual plant, where, as we have seen, present incentives work against adopting or experimenting with the new for fear of disrupting the operation of the old.

Though there is room for improvement, we may expect that growth will continue.

10

The Great Debate

The rule of Stalin brought to the Soviet Union not only rapid economic growth, but also a distressing deep-freeze of thought and initiative in many areas of life. Under Stalin's promptings, the Marxian legacy was to be received with the spirit of blind credulity, and economics, more than any other area of inquiry, became incapable of further scientific development. Stalin's death, however, lifted many of these restraints from intellectual life. The Twentieth Party Congress in 1956 removed the stamp of heresy from the study of western economic analysis and its applications and before long changed the content of economic publications from oppressive sterility into an exciting forum for debate.

Such debate was widespread and frank, and it brought to the fore a number of criticisms of the working of the Soviet economy and at the same time a variety of proposals for reform. Some of these are now the subject of widespread experimentation, others are being put into practice.

I. WEAKNESSES EXAMINED

A. Antiquated Planning Methods and Incentives

One of the most obvious complaints voiced was concerned with the consequences of having successfully established a modern industrialized economy. This *economy was vastly larger and more complex* in the mid-1950s than in 1928, and the unsophisticated material-balance system of planning, relying on successive campaigns to enlarge one bottleneck after another, was regarded as highly inadequate. Not only had the quantities and types of output increased enormously, but the same was true of inputs, whether labor, land, or capital. The system's ability to handle such changes was taxed to the limit. According to A. Efimov, Director of the Economic Research Institute of Gosplan, only first-order iterations could be handled when setting up the Seven-Year Plan. Even that involved 30 million computations for the material balances alone, and only arithmetical "keyboard calculating machines" and "primitive computing technology" were available.

Increasingly, the need was felt to shorten the communication lines between the planning hierarchy, ever growing, and the number of firms, continually growing also. Something, it was argued, had to be done to transmit information and orders with greater speed and fidelity and at lower cost. Without it the economy would respond less and less well to changing conditions of demand and input availability. Worse yet, failing radical reforms in planning methods, argued Victor Glushkov, head of the Soviet research program in cybernetics, the planning bureaucracy would have to grow 36-fold by 1980, to the point of requiring the entire Soviet population! Such a bureaucratic Frankenstein could not be allowed to live.[1] Some kind of improvement or decentralization was becoming indispensable.

In addition to the production of so much more and so many new kinds of goods by so many more firms, the *system of priorities had also changed.* Unlike in 1928, priorities were no longer few and clear. Many more sectors besides pig iron, coal, electricity, cement, and steel were now regarded as important. The top priorities of Stalin, concentrated in basic and heavy industry, were easily plannable, especially when the performance of other sectors was gladly neglected, and thus a cushion was provided to absorb errors. As Premier Khrushchev put it, "steel production is like a much-used road with deep ruts; even a blind horse

---

[1] As a Czech economist put it recently, "socialism is an economic system designed to solve problems which only occur in socialism."

will not lose its way . . . Some officials have put on steel blinkers; they do everything as they were taught in their day. A material appears which is superior to steel and is cheaper but they keep on shouting, 'steel, steel'." [2] Whether blind or not, in the 1950's old-style planning was becoming exceedingly more difficult. At the same time, the types of incentives which served their purpose for enforcing one set of priorities might be bad for another. Soviet agriculture is a case in point of a sector which was increasingly regarded as important, while its terms of trade were still reflecting the desire to "collect that tribute."

The need for thinking seriously about *obsolescence of equipment and the introduction of new technology,* even if old equipment had not yet worn out, was also arising. The abundant labor supply was becoming increasingly scarce, as the effect on the working population of the war years was becoming visible. Therefore, the old time-honored approach of lavishly using labor with any kind of equipment at all was becoming less wise every day. But the present system of incentives, as we saw in Chapter 9, was making no use of the disbursed initiative of managers for innovation and in fact made them most reticent to innovate at all.

Furthermore, the need for centralizing planning on the grounds that *trustworthy and capable leadership personnel* was scarce had disappeared. A well-trained generation of managers and, for that matter, of laborers had replaced an army of ex-peasants. They were being increasingly frustrated by the bureaucratic pressures exerted upon them, stultifying their initiative, penalizing their originality, discouraging their intelligence, and leading them to engage in a number of highly undesirable practices rather than to be obedient executants of the plan. On the other hand, abolishing the bureaucracy and letting enterprise managers make *all* decisions was also not desirable or possible. It was not desirable for fear that the regime's values as to the grand strategy of development might get undermined. It was not possible because any decentralized decision making would have to use prices, and Soviet prices were eminently irrational, capable of supporting only nonsensical decisions.

---

[2] *Pravda,* November 20, 1962, p. 4.

B. Economic Inefficiency

The very fact that the Revolution was a thing of long ago, and that a period of social and political stability had been established, also seemed to favor a return of the quest for *economic efficiency*. Kantorovich, Director of the Laboratory for Economic-Mathematical Methods of the Siberian Department of the Academy of Sciences, argued, for instance, that more rational methods of planning and administration could increase Soviet industrial output by 50% without the use of new inputs. However, planning officials, though drowning in data, were short of the right kind of information needed to make crucial choices on questions of efficiency.

This became especially obvious in the realm of foreign trade. While building "socialism in one country," Stalin had deliberately foregone the advantages of a potential international division of labor. Feeling (quite justifiably) surrounded by a hostile world, the Soviet Union in fact harkened to the old advice of Adam Smith, declaring that defense is more important than opulence. Rather than concentrating production in areas in which the Soviet Union had a comparative advantage, and reaping (as in marginal condition 2 above) the gains from trade through an involved system of international exchanges, Stalin chose autarky— to be safely poor rather than insecurely rich. To be sure, there was some foreign trade, as we have seen when discussing capital goods imports as an aid to growth, but such trade was never looked upon as anything more than a "safety valve." One could import to safeguard fulfillment of the plan, but only as a last resort. Exports, in turn, were a necessary evil to pay for imports. Yet the optimum foreign-trade volume was zero, implying zero dependence on others.

After 1945, when a number of new socialist nations were established in Europe, this Stalinist policy was slavishly copied, together with the whole system of material-balance-type planning. Every single national unit, whether East Germany, Hungary, or Bulgaria, tried to be economically independent of all others, to build up within its borders a complete set of industries. What had been costly, though possible for the richly endowed Soviet Union, however, was suicidal for her new brothers in faith. Just as the residents of Massachusetts would be incredibly poor if they insisted on making everything within their own borders, from cars to bananas to wheat, the populations of the new socialist countries in Eastern Europe must have paid heavily in terms of output foregone for their governments' attempts to create a full complement of industries on the basis of inadequate resource endowments.

After Stalin's death, this was frankly discussed, and many decisions of this sort were reversed. At the same time, it was argued that a grand international division of labor could clearly be of great advantage. The Council for Mutual Economic Aid became the organization of Soviet-bloc countries promoting such experiments. It was pointed out that the socialist countries of 1955, unlike the Soviet Union of 1917, were not fortresses beleaguered by a hostile world, but rather part of a group of friendly states with similar purposes. Though the socialist camp *as a whole* still had to strive for economic independence from the capitalist world, *within* the camp such political consideration did not need to play a role. There was no reason at all why Poland could not produce all the ocean-going vessels for the entire bloc of socialist nations, East Germany all the chemicals, and Czechoslovakia all the trucks, if these were the areas in which their labor, land, and capital could do relatively best. There was no need, in short, to steer away from dependence upon friends.[3]

The discussion of marginal condition 2 in Chapters 2 and 4 illustrates well the possibilities involved. If the marginal rates of transformation (MRT) between busses and locomotives were 2/1 in Hungary and 3/1 in East Germany, for instance, ignoring other countries, East Germany should specialize in busses and Hungary in locomotives. By producing 1 more locomotive, Hungary would have to sacrifice 2 busses, while East Germany could forego production of 1 locomotive, releasing resources for making 3 busses. Yet under Soviet-bloc conditions no such international specialization would occur unless deliberately planned and ex-

---

[3] For a detailed study of the Council for Mutual Economic Aid, its decisions, and how they are made, consult the author's *Economic Integration in the Soviet Bloc: With An East German Case Study* (New York: F. A. Praeger, 1965).

ecuted by the Central Planning Boards. Hungary's national economic planners, for example, would have to cut production and increase imports of busses, while raising production and exports of locomotives. East Germany would do the opposite and, depending on the exact terms of trade, both could be better off after specialization and trade than before, in our case sharing the increased bus output of 1 (or, multiplying all figures by 2, of 2, if you prefer). Unfortunately, planners have been unable to find a criterion for a decision on who has a comparative advantage in what. This may be fairly obvious in some cases (he who has neither iron ore nor coal is unlikely to be best at making steel), but in most cases it is not. The economists' natural inclination would be to compare prices and, *if prices were rational,* this would, indeed, be correct. Given the above MRT's, rational prices should *reflect marginal costs* as follows (subscripts referring to busses and locomotives):

In Hungary,

$$MRT_{b,l} = \frac{2}{1} = \frac{MC_l}{MC_b} = \frac{P_l}{P_b}$$

In East Germany,

$$MRT_{b,l} = \frac{3}{1} = \frac{MC_l}{MC_b} = \frac{P_l}{P_b}$$

Busses would clearly be relatively cheaper in East Germany (costing in money *and* in resources as much as $\frac{1}{3}$ locomotive each) than in Hungary (costing in money *and* resources as much as $\frac{1}{2}$ locomotive each). Locomotives would be seen to be relatively cheaper in Hungary, costing in money *and* resources as much as 2 busses each, rather than 3 busses, as in East Germany. However, as we have seen, prices in the Soviet Union are not rational, being based on *planned* and *adjusted* and *average* costs, *excluding some costs altogether* for ideological reasons. The same is true in other East European countries. Hence the above MRT might be perfectly consistent with the following prices:

	Hungary	East Germany
1 Locomotive	12,000 forint	60,000 DM
1 Bus	3,000 forint	60,000 DM

As a result, anyone within the Council for Mutual Economic Aid, trying to determine international specialization on the basis of prices, could, and in our case would, make a wrong decision. Prices are saying that a locomotive is four times as expensive as a bus in Hungary, and equally as expensive in East Germany. Specialization of Hungary in busses, and of East Germany in locomotives, seems indicated. But *money* costs do not reflect *resource* costs. Such specialization would decrease world output: Hungary can in fact produce another bus not by giving up ¼ locomotive (as prices are saying), but only by giving up ½ locomotive (as marginal costs, not known to planners, indicate). At the same time, East Germany cannot, by not producing a bus, produce a locomotive instead (as prices are suggesting), but she can only produce ⅓ locomotive more (as marginal costs tell us).

In the same way that efficient resource use is made impossible, except by accident, internationally, the absence of rational prices bans efficiency from the internal economy. Whenever a planner or manager decides to use one input rather than another or to make this output rather than that one, or to use this variant of investment rather than that one, he cannot trust prices to help him act in a rational fashion. This has become obvious to many and caused great concern.

II. REMEDIES SUGGESTED

A. *Central Mathematical Planning*

Basically two types of remedies have been suggested for this state of affairs. The first one involves improving the present system of central planning by forging new tools for the central planner. Such tools would be the ones we have become acquainted with in Chapters 7 and 8. Ever since 1956, the possibility of *adopting comprehensive input-output type planning* has been discussed. It might come as a surprise that this has not happened earlier, since input-output analysis seems eminently qualified for the kind of things the Soviets clearly are desirous of achieving. Quite apart from bureaucratic inertia which stands in the way of anything new, this is largely due to an old Marxist taboo, an ingrained doctrinaire hostility to the use of mathematics in economics. However hard this may be to understand, there were in addition practical reasons, such as the low level of mathematical skill of planners and the unavailability of computers.

Some of this has been overcome, and the intellectual respectability of input-output analysis is now established. The fact that Wassily Leontief was born in Russia undoubtedly helped.[4] But most of all, many in present planning circles were deeply impressed by the potential speedy construction, via the inverse matrix and high-speed computers, of a whole number of alternative consistent plans. This compared well, indeed, with the crude single variant plan now constructed, which is never finished on time and is poorly balanced at that. Premier Khrushchev himself complained of the neglect by current planning methods of interdependencies. He compared the system to "a circle . . . divided into 360 degrees," with "these 360 parts . . . all apportioned among committees, ministries, and departments of Gosplan, each of which takes care only of the segment allotted to it." Hence the Soviet government consented to a program designed to catch up with the West in regard to theoretical and empirical work on input-output analysis.

For 1959, a 173-commodity experimental input-output table was established for the Soviet Union.[5] It was found that the existing system did not engender enough information for a more comprehensive table, and that there was the need, in order to go over to input-output planning, to change "from top to bottom" the existing system of accounting and reporting. Even the 1959 table, using one fifth of industrial firms as a sample, was based on estimates rather than the results of systematic account-

---

[4] Nemchinov, then Director of the Laboratory for Economic-Mathematical Methods of the USSR Academy of Sciences, in his *Application of Mathematics in Economic Investigations* (Moscow, 1959) argues that Leontief was inspired by a Soviet 1923–1924 overall "chess-board" balance of the national economy. His work has been published in English as *The Use of Mathematics in Economics* (Edinburgh: Oliver and Boyd, 1964).

[5] By 1964, every Soviet bloc country in Europe, including Yugoslavia, but excluding Albania, had constructed input-output tables. In fact, the most comprehensive ones were those of Poland and Hungary.

ing. A number of other pilot models have also been worked out, such as for the Mordovskoi region and individual smaller territories.

This kind of work has been carried out in a number of places, notably in the new Laboratory for the Use of Statistics and Mathematical Methods in Economics in Novosibirsk, the Economic Research Institute of Gosplan, and the Institute for Electronic Control Machines of the Academy of Sciences.

It must be emphasized that such work is only beginning to gain momentum. Many, including the late Nemchinov, have expressed the belief that input-output analysis will never be more than an auxiliary tool added to the present system. In a sense this will always have to be true. The "perfect computation" discussed in Chapter 8 is utopian. However, a lot more of it could be done than has ever been tried. Yet there are many in the Soviet bureaucracy who shy away from the new technique. This may in part be due to an inflated ego nourishing the belief that with enough practice one day a faultless and exhaustive economic plan can be drawn up with present techniques. More likely, however, it is nourished by the fear that the input-output technique may, in a situation where not all targets can be fulfilled, be more conducive to random cutbacks in all of them rather than to pursuit of the time-honored technique of fulfilling top goals while sacrificing the rest. In addition, the present technique, some argue, assures closer contact between planners and managers than could be maintained by an electronic brain. Be that as it may, there is no reason to expect any *thorough* transformation of the Soviet economy into our model of Chapter 7 any time soon.

This holds even more for the technique of linear programming. So far, its applications have been confined entirely to small problems and individual firms. For instance, the best pattern of rail shipments of coal and cement has been investigated for the Far East and parts of Siberia, a national timber transportation program has been studied as well as the old classic, what types and quantities of food would constitute the optimal diet. Kantorovich and Novozhilov, Professor at the Leningrad Economic-Engineering Institute, have stressed the need for a sound price system to improve planning and have pointed out that a national economic plan reflecting the politically desired final bill of goods, if worked out via linear programming techniques, could provide rational prices as a by-product.[6] Such talk, however, clashes with Marxian dogma and automatically sets many minds against the new approach. To many, determination of shadow prices, reflecting a demand-supply equilibrium, and making decentralized decisions on the basis of such meaningful value parameters, is pure heresy. It is easily seen to have harmful political implications and vicious intent. It contradicts the old bias that planners' wisdom can replace "blind market forces" and that fiats couched in physical terms are superior. This, of course, fails to see that a price system is inherent in *any* system of maximizing against restraints, such as the Soviet attempt to maximize production from given resources. Kantorovich's "objectively conditioned valuations," emerging from an optimum plan, simply prove this fact. And as Kantorovich has pointed out, an optimum plan can be worked out to fulfill *any* set of preferences, including, we may add, those of central planners determined to ignore private consumers.[7]

In summary, the model of central planning discussed in Chapter 8 is even farther from realization than that of Chapter 7. Widespread use of linear programming on a national scale, as a replacement of old fashioned planning tools, is dreamed of by some, but it is music of a very distant future. Ideology as well as insufficiently advanced and insufficiently available computers are to blame for this.

---

[6] See L. V. Kantorovich, *Economic Calculation of the Best Use of Resources* (Moscow 1959). This work has recently been published in English as *The Best Use of Economic Resources* (Cambridge, Massachusetts: Harvard University Press, 1965).

[7] Kantorovich's language itself was undoubtedly anathema to Marxist critics who are sure that use of mathematics and marginalism are equivalent to building on sand. Describing how the planners' computers perform the job of capitalism's "invisible hand," Kantorovich had said: "There evolves in the process of plan construction a *sui generis* 'competitive struggle' between different technological paths accompanied by 'price fluctuations' which help to reveal those whose adoption would be most purposeful." *Op. cit.*, Russian edition, p. 323. Of this we have had a glance in Chapter 8.

B. Decentralization and the Use of Market Forces

This brings us to the second major set of reform proposals. Instead of improving central planning by sharpening the central planners' mathematical tools, it is suggested with an eye to Lange's model (see Chapter 6) that *widespread decentralization* be introduced. This should become possible by *rationalizing the price system*. Very much in the spirit of the Yugoslav Djilas, the advocates of such a move are in effect saying that the Party's objective function of tearing a country loose from backwardness has been fulfilled. If it continued to insist on clumsily guiding every detail of economic life, it would become a parasite. The freedom of managers must be vastly increased and their initiative allowed to be used. All the present problems, they argue, would be alleviated by letting firms follow the profit motive, if only prices were meaningful guides to action.

This type of approach is frequently attributed to Yevsei Liberman, Professor at Kharkov University, whose stirring proposals, made since the mid-1950's, have been published since 1962 in *Pravda*. He argues that managers should be given as few instructions from the central authorities as possible and be judged by the *profit* they make *in relation to the capital* they have. Firms should be asked to make a consistent and feasible proposal as to what they want to produce, how and when, subject to planners' approval. Hence planning would occur "from the bottom up." For fulfilling the approved plan, management and labor would receive a bonus based on actual profit, if the profit plan is fulfilled or underfulfilled. The bonus would be based on some figure between actual and plan profits, if the plan were overfulfilled. This would encourage high proposed plan targets and all-out efforts to economize on inputs and maximize high-quality salable output. Plans should also be long-term so as to encourage technical innovation and assure to managers that they will benefit from it. The Central Planning Board would continue to determine the major proportions of economic activity and channel major investments into sectors desired by it. For the scheme to work, prices, of course, would have to be rational. Otherwise, producing the most valuable output and using the cheapest inputs would make no sense.

Just as Kantorovich and Novozhilov, Liberman and his followers were accused of antisocialist tricks, since it is extremely difficult for most to disassociate use of rational prices for efficiency's sake from the capitalist institutions with which market prices have been historically connected. Nevertheless, as with input-output and linear programming techniques, tentative and hesitant moves towards experimenting with a market model are being taken. In several geographic locations in 1964, Soviet retail stores were allowed to contract directly with factories of their own choice. This was limited to the textile, leather, shoe, and garment sectors. To increase the quality of consumer goods and to encourage the production of correct assortments, producing firms' production plans were only regarded as fulfilled if output was acceptable to retail outlets. In late 1965, a new Soviet law, while increasing the powers of Gosplan at the expense of some territorial planning agencies which were abolished, also increased the powers of all managers for day-to-day operations. They can now decide for themselves the number of workers they need and the type and amount of their remuneration. They can also make independent decisions about how to invest circulating funds for productive purposes or for the benefit of employees.

C. The Need for Price Reform

On the other hand, for all those hopeful of a radical price reform, assuring rationality, the July 1, 1963 industrial price revision in the USSR was a great setback. It constituted a complete victory for the traditionalists, such as Maizenberg (Deputy Chief of the Gosplan Price Bureau), Ostrovitianov (the Academician), Gatovskii (Chief editor of Voprosy Ekonomiki), and Turetskii (Professor at the Moscow Institute of National Economy). The principle of price setting, as we discussed it in the previous chapter, remained unchanged. Only the structure of industrial wholesale prices was changed, by restoring normal profit to all branches (ratifying in effect uneven changes in costs and productivity over the past years) and by making depreciation rates more realistic. Retail, agricultural procurement, and foreign trade prices were unaffected. Even those potential reformers, who wanted to stay closer to the Marxian framework and add a charge onto Marx's $c + v$, proportional everywhere to wages, v (Strumilin, the Academician, and Kronrod, Chief of the Sector of Political Economy of the Institute of Economics of the Academy of Sciences) or capital invested (Malyshev, Deputy Chief of the Central Statistical Administration and Vaag, of Gosplan) or $c + v$ itself (Kondrashev of the Institute of Economics of the Academy of Sciences) were not accommodated.

III. EXPERIMENTS OUTSIDE THE USSR

Other, sometimes truly large-scale, experiments with "new systems of economic planning and management" are being conducted in all other East European socialist countries. All of them have the same goals of pruning the bureaucracy and encouraging, via production for profit, the production of the right kinds of goods in good quality and the speedy application of the latest technology. In Bulgaria, the "new system" was tested in fifty enterprises since April 1964, and the test was greatly expanded in 1965. By the end of that year, industrial plants employing a third of the industrial labor force and producing 44% of industrial output had gone over to the new system. So had trade enterprises handling 30% of turnover. The test is to be concluded at the end of 1966, and "beginning in 1967" the new model is scheduled for "application *on basic lines* in the whole national economy." Eventually, the CPB is still to determine physical targets for basic inputs and outputs, the size of capital formation and collective consumption, technical progress, foreign trade and a number of financial factors (including wages). There is to be a *three-price system:* fixed prices set by the center for basic goods and important consumer goods, guided prices set by firms within centrally determined minima and maxima for other goods, and free prices set by supply and demand for the rest. A complete price reform is planned for the future. Guidelines published in December 1965 indicate that future prices will have to cover a number of taxes to be imposed upon firms, including a "tax" on fixed and working capital in hand (that is, an interest charge) and a "tax" on agricultural, forestry, and extractive industry firms whose income is being influenced by varying natural conditions (that is, a rent charge). The "tax" on capital is to be 2% for some and 5% for most enterprises, and is to be based on a capital stock to be newly evaluated. Enterprises are to be financially self-supporting and, except for heavy industry which is to continue to get budget grants, they are to finance investment from their own funds or interest-bearing bank loans. In general, each firm is to have increased independence, initiative, and responsibility, making its own Five-Year Plan and annual plan, but taking into consideration central norms and being subject to central correction, if the sum of individual plans is contrary to national possibilities or the public interest. All this is clearly much too vague to allow anything more than a wild guess as to what is really going to happen.

Czechoslovakia contemplates similar changes, but the reforms are labeled a "long-range, complicated political process," going beyond 1970. Starting in 1966, the three-price system is also being introduced. Measured by production volume in 1966, 64% of all goods will have fixed prices, 29% guided prices, and 7% free prices. Wholesale prices, including an interest charge, are to be completely revised by 1968.

Hungary plans economic reforms of like nature, to be implemented over three years (as of November 1965). Apart from nationally important investments, however, complete *abandonment,* rather than reduction, of compulsory centrally directed indices is contemplated, with enterprises determining output completely independently with the aim of profit maximization. There will be no administrative guidance from the center at all, only guidance by economic levers, that is, again the three-price system. In early 1966, in the midst of complaints that the 5% interest charge on all capital introduced in 1964 was not yet reflected anywhere in prices, a number of price revisions were being undertaken. However, all measures for 1966 and 1967 were seen as only partial, the full implementation of the new model having to await the 1968 general industrial price revision.

By early 1966, similar price and administrative revisions had occurred or were scheduled as a result of similar debates in the other East European socialist countries. In most cases, the revisions or plans thereof went further towards establishing rationality than did the Soviet Union. In East Germany and

Poland, too, an interest charge on capital invested was introduced or announced as imminent, a remarkably un-Marxian achievement. In all cases, the new system was not scheduled to be fully in effect until the late 1960's. Even in the Soviet Union, charging of interest was openly advocated by more and more, as by Academician V. A. Trapeznikov. In addition, the charging of rent for the use of natural resources such as minerals, land, water, and forests has been vigorously promoted by V. Shkatov of Gosplan and Malyshev. Premier Kosygin, in late 1965, promised completely new prices for 1967–1968.

IV. SUMMARY

To conclude our discussion of the Great Debate, we can state that there has been groping for new approaches in planning and management of the economy with ever increasing intensity. But it is also true that *highly conservative paths of reform have been preferred* and the new has by no means swept the field. The goal has been neither to make the power of the center complete nor to give it up altogether. Rather there has been search for the "proper" combination of central direction with the maximum scope for power, initiative, and responsibility at the local level.

Nowhere were the nasty skeletons of Marxian dogma completely swept away. The debate may have paved the way, but vested interests prevented *so far* any radical changes. It is undoubtedly too much to expect this. Certainly the fact that radical ideas can now be openly discussed and even experimented with, which a little over a decade ago would have been unthinkable, is reason for hope.[8]

Possibly the postwar attitude of Oskar Lange will point the way to the future. He argued that Marxism must be preserved as a compass for interpreting the broad sweep of history, but that economic science in the mature socialist economy might just as well borrow as much as possible from the modern

___
[8] Although the Soviet government is by no means committed to the radical changes proposed by them, it awarded the Lenin Prize to Nemchinov, Kantorovich, and Novozhilov in 1965.

"bourgeois" techniques developed since the death of Marx. As the awareness of economic inefficiency grows, this is likely to be the case. Yet Soviet and other socialist leaders are highly sensitive to claims of "bourgeois degeneration" of their economies, and they can be expected to go slow with reforms. Whether the future socialist countries look more like the Lange-esque world of Chapter 6 or the computerized one of Chapters 7 and 8 remains to be seen.[9]

---

[9] The reader unable to read the original sources may wish to consult the *Press Surveys* and *Situation Reports* on Eastern Europe regularly published in mimeographed form by the research departments of Radio Free Europe or the *Current Digest of the Soviet Press.*

11

An All-Important Question

Another thing that remains to be seen is what will happen to the relative importance of socialist and capitalist economies in the world. Some have suggested that these two types of economic organization may well converge and eventually be indistinguishable from one another. It is easy to see how this view may be acquired.

We have already seen how neither capitalist nor socialist reality corresponds to the textbook models we have studied in Chapter 4 on the one hand and Chapters 6–8 on the other. Governments in capitalist countries are distressed because their economies, left to themselves, do not achieve in any satisfactory manner the four goals outlined in Chapters 2 and 3. As a result, they play larger and larger roles in economic life. The typical response of some governments, such as that of the United States, has been shown briefly in Chapter 5. Other capitalist governments, however, use other means. France is engaging, for instance, in a large-scale experiment of "indicative," that is, noncoercive, planning. A General Plan Commission makes long-term (5 to 10 year) projections of final demands (our columns 4–7, Table 7-1). With the help of an input-output model, it then projects "gross output targets" (our column 8, Table 7-1). These are submitted to committees of private businessmen, including some trade-union officials and civil servants. They comment on the "plan," and the General Commissioner might subsequently alter it in view of such comments. Ultimately the "plan" is sent to Parliament and published. However, it does *not* impose an obligation on anyone, nor does it imply government sanction for what it thinks is going to happen. The whole idea is to make a *consistent forecast of likely changes,* and the business community seems to favor such reduction in uncertainty. France certainly has had, whether because of this or not, a remarkable record of full employment and rapid growth in recent years.[1]

Countries of the underdeveloped world are similarly interested in input-output analysis. By comparing the structure of a developed economy with that of their own via input-output tables, they can pinpoint gaps in their own structure, as well as the widespread consequences of any change predicted. Though this by itself will not bring about development, an attempt to imitate the structure of developed economies, provided the necessary resource endowment is potentially available, will probably be the best course of action, and progress along a well-mapped road is likely to be fastest.[2]

While this kind of government activity within the framework of essentially private-enterprise economies is likely to increase, we saw in Chapter 10 how the East European socialist countries are groping for increased use of market forces. No wonder then, if some seem to detect a movement toward convergence. Every country in the world, by deliberate choice or by default, is in fact choosing one of the models of economic organization discussed in this book or some mixture of them, even if none will ever realize such models in all their purity. In fact, it is not hard to guess that the underdeveloped and politically uncommitted nations of this world will be eclectic, choosing from the "capitalist West" and the "socialist East" whatever features seem to serve their purposes best. Anyone who has carefully studied this book can look at any country in the world, be it India, China, West

---

[1] This example of the use of input-output analysis serves to illustrate once more how value-free this analysis is. It tells us where the economy is and is likely to go, not where it should be. A 1961 Geneva conference on input-output analysis, for example, was attended by 41 countries, mostly nonsocialist.

[2] See the interesting article by Wassily Leontief, "The Structure of Development," *Scientific American,* September 1963, pp. 148 ff.

Germany, Sweden, or Brazil, and he will be able to place them somewhere within the framework of organizational models we have discussed. The details will differ but the fundamental economic problem is the same everywhere.

I. WHAT OF FREEDOM AND HUMAN DIGNITY?

There remains one large final question that should be dealt with. We have studied the various means of achieving *economic* welfare, and we have concentrated on the achievement of one or any of these: full and efficient use of resources and "desirable" distribution and growth rate of output. Even though the economist, *as an economist,* cannot say more, as a human being he can and, this author believes, he should. Given the various means of achieving the above goals, do they all have the same effects on noneconomic welfare? What are the implications for the quality of human life supported by the various forms of organization? Above all, what do they imply about human freedom and human dignity? This is a most important question, for this author believes that the real challenge of the 20th century to man is not to solve the problem of scarcity, but for free men to act courageously to withstand the totalitarian onslaught directed to acquire title to this entire planet. *How* we deal with the problem of scarcity, however, may well influence significantly the outcome of that larger struggle.

The *abolition* of the market mechanism in favor of a "conscious" direction of the economy by a socialistic government possibly restrains the sphere of individual freedom.[3] As has happened in Eastern Europe, the attempt to break the despotism of physical want has chained man to the despotism of those wielding arbitrary power. Except for the half-hearted socialism of Scandinavia and Great Britain, the maintenance of socialism by democratic means, as once envisaged by Oskar Lange, has remained a utopia. This is a brute fact. As Friedrich von Hayek has stated so well,[4] the large-scale central direction of economic activity on behalf

---

[3] In much of the underdeveloped world this may, however, not be the case at all.

[4] See his *The Road to Serfdom* (Chicago: University of Chicago Press 1944).

of a definite social goal, if it is to be maintained, will have to oppress individual freedom whenever it is an obstacle to the execution of the plan. All resources will have to be organized for the unitary end, for the "common good," and an autonomous sphere where the individual reigns supreme cannot be recognized. Just as a military campaign cannot be planned and carried out by democratic procedure, because parts of it are bound to be inconsistent, the central planner, who really wants to get things done, cannot be hampered by democratic fetters. As in the Soviet Union with economic growth, the single-minded pursuit of any one goal requires much effective coercion which is best provided by dictatorship. Then being controlled in matters economic comes to mean being controlled in everything. And the power given to a few for reasons economic provides the opportunity for ambitious men to institute a bloody tyranny and to engage in excesses quite unnecessary to achieve the original goals. Maybe socialism does not *have* to involve dictatorship (Stalin really *is* dead, and the USSR is *not* accurately described as a slave state ruled by professional criminals), but we should keep in mind that it might.

This author would certainly prefer to live in a society which attaches great value to the human personality. Such importance attributed to an individual is notably absent in a totalitarian state. The individual is no longer important in his own right, but only insofar as he serves the state. Initially, the vision of losing one's individuality in pursuit of a common ideal is attractive to many. Yet all too often men become possessed by a vision, abandon humanity, and treat their fellows abominably. Yet the above should not be interpreted as a plea for *laissez-faire* and complete government abstention from intervention in economic life. There is more than one path to salvation. There is no need to tolerate present socialist inhumanities for the sake of future wealth, to annihilate in the name of love. Nor is there need to be helpless before the vagaries of uncontrolled capitalist markets. *Correction* of the market mechanism, as we discussed it in Chapter 5, however short it leaves us of perfection, seems to this author eminently necessary as well as superior to socialism, because it implies less concentration of power in the hands of a few and, therefore, a much lesser sacrifice of noneconomic welfare while potentially achieving at least as much of our economic goals. It may be argued that the market mechanism, subtly and effectively controlled by appropriate government intervention, is just another way of inducing or bribing people into doing what is for the "common good." Hence people have only the illusion of being free. Following the carrot, rather than running from the stick, people only *feel* more free! Maybe that is so. But illusion or not, this author would argue, it makes all the difference in the world. This gentle control can set the framework within which individual man can find the possibility of expressing his innate potentialities to the fullest, where he needs neither to be destroyed by others nor to destroy them, where he can come to know, respect, and relate with his fellow man on equal terms.

If we can live through the present period and prevent the age of worldwide tyranny from being born, mankind may yet reach maturity, where it emerges from the abyss of divisiveness and suffering and becomes united on the basis of the sacredness of each human person. To help bring that about is the challenge of the 20th century to each one of us.

BIBLIOGRAPHY

Ames, Edward. *Soviet Economic Processes* (Homewood: Irwin, 1965).
Balassa, Bela A. *The Hungarian Experience in Economic Planning* (New Haven: Yale University Press, 1959).
Bergson, Abram. "Socialist Economics," *American Economic Association, A Survey of Contemporary Economics*, Howard S. Ellis, ed. (Philadelphia: The Blakiston Company, 1948).
Bornstein, Morris. "The Soviet Price System," *American Economic Review*, March 1962, pp. 64 ff. "The Soviet Price Reform Discussion," *Quarterly Journal of Economics*, February 1964, pp. 15 ff.
Boulding, K. E. "Welfare Economics," *American Economic Association, A Survey of Contemporary Economics*, Bernard F. Haley, ed. (Homewood: Irwin, 1952).
———. *Principles of Economic Policy* (Englewood Cliffs, New Jersey: Prentice-Hall, 1958), especially Chapters 4 and 6.
———. *The Meaning of the Twentieth Century* (New York: Harper and Row, 1964).
Campbell, Robert W. *Soviet Economic Power* (Cambridge, Massachusetts: The Riverside Press, 1960).
Chenery, Hollis B., and Clark, Paul G. *Interindustry Economics* (New York: John Wiley and Sons, 1962).
Goldman, Marshall I. "Economic Controversy in the Soviet Union," *Foreign Affairs*, April 1963, pp. 498 ff.
Grossman, Gregory. "Scarce Capital and Soviet Doctrine," *Quarterly Journal of Economics*, August 1953, pp. 311 ff.
———. *Value and Plan* (Berkeley: University of California Press, 1960).
———. "Notes for a Theory of the Command Economy," *Soviet Studies*, October 1963, pp. 101 ff.
Hayek, F. A. von. "Socialist Calculation: The Competitive 'Solution'," *Economica*, May 1940, pp. 125 ff.
———. *The Road to Serfdom* (Chicago: University of Chicago Press, 1944).

————. *Collectivist Economic Planning* (London: Routledge and Kegan Paul, 1963).

Holzman, Franklyn D., ed. *Readings on the Soviet Economy* (Chicago: Rand McNally and Company, 1962), especially David Granick, "An Organizational Model of Soviet Industrial Planning,"

   Herbert S. Levine, "The Centralized Planning of Supply in Soviet Industry,"

   Joseph S. Berliner, "The Informal Organization of the Soviet Firm,"

   ————. "Managerial Incentives and Decision-making: A Comparison of the United States and the Soviet Union."

Jasny, Naum. "A Note on Rationality and Efficiency in the Soviet Economy," *Soviet Studies,* April 1961, pp. 353 ff, and July 1961, pp. 35 ff.

Kaser, M. C. "Soviet Planning and the Price Mechanism," *Economic Journal,* March 1950, pp. 81 ff.

Kantorovich, L. V. *Economic Calculation of the Best Use of Resources* (Moscow, 1959), published as *The Best Use of Economic Resources* (Cambridge, Massachusetts: Harvard University Press, 1965).

Köhler, Heinz. *Economic Integration in the Soviet Bloc: With An East German Case Study* (New York: F. A. Praeger, 1965).

Koopmans, Tjalling C. "Efficient Allocation of Resources," *Econometrica,* October 1951, pp. 455 ff.

Lange, Oskar. "Marxian Economics and Modern Economic Theory," *Review of Economic Studies,* June 1935, pp. 189 ff.

————. "The Foundations of Welfare Economics," *Econometrica,* July-October 1942, pp. 215 ff.

————. "Marxian Economics in the Soviet Union," *American Economic Review,* March 1945, pp. 127 ff.

————. "The Practice of Economic Planning and the Optimum Allocation of Resources," *Econometrica.* Supplement July 1949, pp. 166 ff.

————, and Taylor, Fred M. *On the Economic Theory of Socialism,* (New York: McGraw Hill, 1964).

Leontief, Wassily. "The Decline and Rise of Soviet Economic Science," *Foreign Affairs,* January 1960, pp. 261 ff.

————. "The Structure of Development," *Scientific American,* September 1963, pp. 148 ff.

Lerner, A. P. "Economic Theory and Socialist Economy," *Review of Economic Studies,* October 1934, pp. 51 ff.

————. "A Note on Socialist Economics," *Review of Economic Studies,* October 1936, pp. 72 ff.

————. "From Vulgar Political Economy to Vulgar Marxism," *Journal of Political Economy,* August 1939, pp. 557 ff.

————. *Everybody's Business* (New York: Harper and Row, 1961).

————. *The Economics of Control* (New York: Macmillan, 1962).

Levine, Herbert S. "Input-Output Analysis and Soviet Planning," *American Economic Review,* May 1962, pp. 127 ff.

Lipsey, R. G. and Lancaster, K. "The General Theory of the Second Best," *Review of Economic Studies,* 1, pp. 11 ff (1956).

McManus, M. "Comments on the General Theory of the Second Best," *Review of Economic Studies*, 1, pp. 11 ff (1956).

Miernyk, William H. *The Elements of Input-Output Analysis* (New York: Random House, 1965).

Nemchinov, V. "Mathematics and Electronics in the Service of Planning," *Problems of Economics*, November 1961, pp. 3 ff.

———. *The Use of Mathematics in Economics* (Edinburgh: Oliver and Boyd, 1964).

Nove, Alec. "The Problem of 'Success Indicators' in Soviet Industry," *Economica*, February 1958.

———. *The Soviet Economy* (New York: Praeger, 1961).

———. "The U.S.S.R.: Myths and Realities," *Lawrence Journal World*, January 21, 1963.

———. "The Liberman Proposals," *Survey*, April 1963, pp. 112 ff.

———. "Economic Trends and Prospects in the U.S.S.R. and Eastern Europe," *American Economic Review*, May 1963, pp. 541 ff.

———. *Economic Rationality and Soviet Politics* (New York: F. A. Praeger, 1964).

Smolinski, Leon. "What next in Soviet Planning?" *Foreign Affairs*, July 1964, pp. 602 ff.

Spulber, Nicolas. *The Soviet Economy* (New York: W. W. Norton, 1962).

United Nations. *Economic Bulletin for Europe*, Vol. 12, No. 1, pp. 57 ff (1960).

Wiles, P. J. D. "Scarcity, Marxism, and Gosplan," *Oxford Economic Papers*, October 1953, pp. 288 ff.

———. "Growth versus Choice," *Economic Journal*, June 1956, pp. 244 ff.

Zauberman, Alfred. "New Winds in Soviet Planning," *Soviet Studies*, July 1960, pp. 1 ff.

———. "The Present State of Soviet 'Planometrics'," *Soviet Studies*, July 1962, pp. 62 ff.

———. "The Soviet and Polish Quest for a Criterion of Investment Efficiency," *Economica*, August 1962, pp. 234 ff.

Index

Activity (in linear programming), 107–121
Additivity, 115
Adjoint matrix, 98
Agricultural prices, 133
Allocation, of goods, optimum, 8–11, 23–25, 47–48, 51, 102, 135
of resources, optimum, 15–17, 49, 103
Antitrust legislation, 55
Assortment of output, 140
Autarky, 147
Authoritarianism, 81, 82, 162–164
Average costs, 39, 41, 70, 73, 132
Average rate of transformation, 15

Barone, E., 67, 69, 80
Beethoven, 33
Blat, 139
Bonus system, 137–141
Borrowing, for efficiency, 23–25
Bukharin, 124
Bulgaria, 147, 156
Bureaucratization, in competitive socialism, 78
in Soviet Union, 140

Capital, as input, defined, 3
formation, 86, 93, 94, 141
goods, 53, 57, 70, 71, 77

Capital *(cont.)*
see also Investment and interest rates; and Growth
Capitalism, defined, 4
perfectly competitive model, 36–53
reality, 54–66
Capital-output ratio, 142
Central Committee, 127
Central Planning Board, in authoritarian socialist models, 82–122
in competitive socialism, 68, 70, 71, 73, 76, 78, 80
in Soviet Union, 127–129, 138–141, 151–152, 154
Cheating, by managers, 79, 80
Cofactor, 96–98
Collective consumption, 61, 62, 64, 77, 80, 81, 93, 94
Collective farm, 126, 133, 135, 136
Colley, A., 54
Column vector, 109
Computers, 45, 94, 95, 102, 122, 145, 151, 152
Constant cost industry, 72
Constant returns to scale, 103, 107, 116
Constraint (in linear programming), 106

Consumer, choice, 134
cooperatives, 133
goods, 53, 57, 70, 71, 77, 133
sovereignty, 41, 76, 134
Consumption, collective, 61, 62, 64, 77, 80, 81, 93, 94
Control figures, 128
Convergence (of capitalism and socialism), 160
Cost, and input-output table, 86
average, 39, 41, 70, 73, 132
fixed, 41
opportunity, 12, 121
total, 39, 70
see also Marginal cost
Council for Mutual Economic Aid, 148–150
Council of Ministers, 127
Czechoslovakia, 157

Dantzig, 106
Demand, in competitive socialism, 73–76
in perfect competition, 38, 40–43
research, 135
Depreciation, 86, 131–132, 139, 155
Derived activity, 115–121
Determinant, defined, 96
second order, 96
third-order, 97
Diminishing returns, 16, 18, 60
Disutility, 22, 23, 42, 51–53
Djilas, 154
Draft plan, 128

East Germany, 147, 157, 158
Economic system, as determining productivity, 4
goals of, 4, 5, 6–35, 45–53
Efficiency, defined, 7
in authoritarian socialism, 102–122
in competitive socialism, 77
in real world capitalism, 55, 56, 77
in Soviet Union, 141, 147–150, 154–156

Efficiency *(cont.)*
seven marginal conditions of, 7–26
under perfect competition, 47–53
Efimov, A., 145
Employment, *see* Full employment; and Unemployment
Equal-product curve, 19, 119
Equilibrium, market price, 40–46
unemployment and, 45–46, 54
Exploitation, 130–132
Externalities, of consumption, 62, 64–66, 77, 78
of production, 62–64, 77, 78

Factor (of production), *see* Inputs
Factor market, 36, 42–46, 52, 53
in competitive socialism, 69, 70, 76
in Soviet Union, 134
Final demand sector, 86, 87, 90, 91, 94, 99, 101, 102
Firms, in authoritarian socialism, 90–93, 102, 103, 121
in competitive socialism, 69
in real capitalism, 55
in Soviet Union, 128, 132–141
under perfect competition, 36, 39, 42–44, 48–53
First World War, 124
Fiscal policy, 54, 55, 57, 77
Five-Year Plan, 126
Fixed costs, 41
France, 160–161
Freedom and socialism, 80, 162–164
Full employment, defined, 6–7
in capitalism, 54
in Soviet Union, 141
under authoritarian socialism, 93
under competitive socialism, 77
under perfect competition, 45–46

Gatovskii, 155
General equilibrium, 44, 45, 67
Glushkov, V., 145
Goals (of Economic Systems), 4, 5–35, 45–53
Goods, defined, 2

Goods market, 36, 38, 40–41, 52
  in competitive socialism, 69, 70, 73–76
  in Soviet Union, 132–135
Gosplan, *see* Central Planning Board in Soviet Union
Government intervention, in capitalism, 54–56, 58, 61–63, 65, 66, 160, 161, 163, 164
Great Britain, 162
Gross national income, 87
Gross national product, 87
Growth, in authoritarian socialism, 93, 94
  in competitive socialism, 70, 77
  in imperfect competition, 57–58
  in perfect competition, 53
  in Soviet Union, 124–126, 141–143
  of output, 33–35

Haveman, R., 55, 61
Hayek, F. A., 67, 68, 78, 79, 162
Hiding (of productive capacity), 138
Hoarding, 138–139
Households, in authoritarian socialism, 82, 102
  in competitive socialism, 69–71
  in real capitalism, 55
  in Soviet Union, 133–135
  under perfect competition, 36, 38, 42–44, 47, 48, 50–53
Hungary, 147, 157

Identity matrix, 95, 98
Incentives, and income distribution, 33, 77
  in competitive socialism, 69–72, 77–80
  in real world capitalism, 55
  in Soviet Union, 134–141, 146
  under authoritarian socialism, 121
  under perfect competition, 38, 42, 48–52
Income distribution, 27–33
  and Marxism, 130

Income distribution *(cont.)*
  in authoritarian socialism, 94
  in competitive socialism, 77, 78
  in perfect competition, 53
  in real world capitalism, 56–57
  in Soviet Union, 141
Increasing cost industry, 72
Increasing returns, 58, 59, 77
Indifference curve, 11, 22
Inflation, 58
Initiative, in authoritarian socialism, 105
  in competitive socialism, 78
  see also Incentives
Input-coefficient matrix, 95
Input-output analysis, 83–105, 150–152, 160–161
Input-output table, 83–88, 91–94, 101, 127, 128
  in Eastern Europe, 151
  in France, 160–161
Inputs, defined, 3
  fixed, 39
  intermediate, 85, 86
  optimum combinations of, 17–19, 50, 103
  optimum utilization of, 21–23, 51, 103
  primary, 85–87, 93–94
  variable, 39
Interdependence, 44, 45, 67, 83, 90–102
  see also Input-output analysis
Interest rates, 46, 86
  and Marxian ideology, 130–132
  in Bulgaria, 156–157
  in competitive socialism, 69–71, 77
  in Czechoslovakia, 157
  in East Germany, 157–158
  in Hungary, 157
  in Poland, 158
  in Soviet Union, 132, 139, 158
International division of labor, 147–150
Inverse matrix, 95, 96, 151
Inversion of matrix, 95–99

Investment and interest rates, 46
 competitive socialism and, 70, 77,
  80–81
 see also Capital; and Growth
Iso-product curve, 19, 119
Iteration, 90–94, 145

Kantorovich, L. V., 106, 147, 152,
  153, 155, 158
Khrushchev, N., 145, 151
Knopf, K., 55, 61
Knowledge, in authoritarian social-
  ism, 94, 102, 104
 in competitive socialism, 80
 in real capitalism, 55
 under perfect competition, 37
Köhler, H., 148
Kolkhoz market, 135, 136
Kondrashev, 156
Koopmans, T. C., 106, 121
Kosygin, A., 158
Kronrod, 156
Kulaks, 126

Labor, as input, defined, 3
 dead, 130–132
 in the Soviet Union, 134
 live, 130–132
 marginal disutility of, 22, 42
Labor theory of value, 130–132
Lancaster, K., 55
Land, as input, defined, 3
Lange, O., 69, 72, 76–79, 82, 132,
  142, 154, 158, 159, 162
Leisure, 22
Lending, for efficiency, 23–25
Lenin, 124, 125
Leontief matrix, 95, 99, 100, 102
Leontief, Wassily, 83, 151, 161
Liberman, Y., 154, 155
Linear programming, 106–122, 152–
  153
Lipsey, R. G., 55
Lysenko, T., 143

Maizenberg, 155

Malyshev, 156
Managers, in Soviet Union, 137–
  141, 146, 154
 of enterprises, in competitive socialism, 69, 70, 77, 79, 80
 of industries, 70–73, 76, 80
 see also Incentives
Marginal conditions of efficiency,
  defined, 8–26
 fulfillment, 47–53
 nonfulfillment in capitalism, 55–
  56
  in socialism, 102–103, 135, 148–
  149
Marginal cost, 12, 21, 39, 41, 48–
  52, 60, 61, 70, 73, 102, 132,
  149, 150
 private versus social, 62–65
Marginal disutility, 22, 23, 42, 51–
  53
Marginal physical product, 17, 19,
  22, 39, 42, 49–53, 59, 103,
  121
Marginal rate of substitution, 8–11,
  17–26
Marginal rate of transformation, 11–
  17, 19–22, 102, 149
Marginal revenue, 39
Marginal utility, 9, 11, 21–25, 28–
  33, 38, 47, 48, 50–52, 63,
  73, 102
 private versus social, 64, 65
Market, economy, 36
 see also Factor market; and Goods
  market
Marx, K., 130–132, 156, 159
Marxism, and Soviet development,
  123
 and Soviet planning, 151, 153, 158
 and Soviet prices, 129–132, 155
 and Stalin, 144
Material balances, 127, 128, 134,
  141, 145
Matrix, adjoint, 98
 defined, 95

Matrix *(cont.)*
  identity, 95, 98
  inverse, 95, 96, 151
  Leontief, 95, 99, 100, 102
  multiplication, 98
  of input coefficients, 95
  subtraction, 95
Matrix inversion, 95–99
Merit standard, 27–28
Michelangelo, 33
Minor, 96, 97
Mises, Ludwig von, 68, 69, 72
Mobility, in real capitalism, 55
  in Soviet Union, 134
  under perfect competition, 37
Monetary policy, 54, 57, 58, 136
Money supply, 46, 57, 58
Monopolist, 55, 57, 77
Monopsonist, 55

Need standard, 28–33
Nemchinov, 151, 152, 158
New Economic Policy, 124, 125
New systems of economic planning
    and management, 156–158
Newton, 33
Novoshilov, 152, 155, 158

Obsolescence, 146
Opportunity cost, 12, 121
Ostrovitianov, 155
Output, assortment, 140
  equitable distribution of, 27–33,
    53, 56–57, 77, 78, 94, 130,
    141
  sufficient growth of, 33–35, 53, 57–
    58, 70, 77, 93, 94, 141–143
  see also Production
Output-capital ratio, 142
Overordering, 138–139

Pareto, V., 7
Pareto optimum, 25, 55
Party directives, 127
Peasants in Soviet Union, 124–126,
    133–137

Perfect competition, assumptions,
    36–38
  efficiency and, 47–53
  employment and, 45–46
  growth and, 53
  income distribution and, 53
  markets, 38–44
  real world and, 55, 60, 61–66
Peter the Great, 123
Planning, centrally (models), 82–
    122
  decentralized, 67–81, 154–155
  indicative, 160–161
  in Soviet Union, 126–129, 150–
    153
Poland, 158
Preobrazhenskii, 125
Price reforms, in Bulgaria, 156
  in Czechoslovakia, 157
  in Hungary, 157
  in Soviet Union, 155–156, 158
Price system, 44–45
  rational, 52–53, 61–62, 64, 68, 73,
    76, 121, 150, 152–154
Prices, as parameter, 40–43, 48–53,
    70
  downward rigidities, 54
  in competitive socialism, 70–73,
    76, 77
  in Soviet Union, 129–135, 155–156
  influenced by firm, 55, 60, 80
  shadow, 121–122, 153
  under perfect competition, 37–42
Processing sector, 85–88, 90, 99,
    101, 102
Production, optimum direction of,
    19–21, 50, 103, 135
  see also Output
Production function, 17, 22
Production possibility curve, 14
Productive process, 3, 4
Profit, in competitive socialism, 69,
    71, 73, 76, 77
  in Marxism, 130–131
  in Soviet Union, 132, 155

Profit maximization, in Hungary, 157
  under authoritarian socialism, 121
  under competitive socialism, 70, 72
  under perfect competition, 39, 48–52, 60, 61
Profit motive, 38, 42, 154
Pure Economics, 2

Quality (of output), 140

Rate of substitution, marginal, 8–11, 17–26
Rate of transformation, average, 15
  marginal, 11–17, 19–22, 102, 149
Rent, 86
  in Bulgaria, 156–157
  in competitive socialism, 69, 71, 77
  in Marxism, 130–132
  in Soviet Union, 132, 158
Resources, *see* Inputs
Retail prices, 133–135
Retained corporate earnings, 57
Returns to scale, 16, 18, 58–60, 77, 103, 107, 116
Revenue, 39

Scandinavia, 162
Scarcity, 2, 52, 94
Second World War, 137
Seven-Year Plan, 145
Shadow prices, 121–122, 153
Shkatov, V., 158
Simplex method, 110–115
Smith, Adam, 147
Social Dividend, 71, 77
Social goods, 61, 62, 66, 71
  see also Collective consumption
Socialism, centralized models of, 82–122
  competitive model of, 67–81
  critique of capitalism by, 58–66
  defined, 4
  in Soviet Union, 123–143
  reform proposals for, 144–159

Socially necessary labor, 131, 132
Soviet economy, 123–143
  growth, 124–126, 141–143
  incentives, 136–141
  performance, 141–143
  planning mechanism, 126–129
  prices, 132–136
  reform proposals, 150–156
  role of Marxism, 130–132
  strategy of development, 123–126
  weaknesses, 144–150
Soviet Revolution, 123
Specialization, as determining productivity, 3
  optimum, 11–14, 48–49, 102, 135, 148–149
Stalin, 125, 126, 144, 145, 147, 148, 162
State Bank, 129, 136
State farms, 133, 136
Strumilin, 156
Subsidies, 55, 57, 64, 65
Substitution, 8–11, 17–26
Supply, in competitive socialism, 73–76
  in perfect competition, 39–44
Surplus value, 131–132

Taxes, 55, 57, 58, 63, 65, 71, 133
Taylor, F. M., 69
Technical coefficients, 67, 68
  assumed constancy of, 103–115, 127
  direct, 88–91, 94, 95, 100, 103
  total, 99
  variable, 107, 115–121
Technical efficiency, 59, 116–118
Technology, and growth in Soviet Union, 139, 140, 142–143, 146
  as determining productivity, 3, 57
  copying, 142
Theory of the second best, 55
Three-price system, 156–157
Total cost, 39, 70
Total revenue, 39

Transactions Table, 83–88, 91–94, 101, 127, 128
Transformation, *see* Rate of
Trapeznikov, V. A., 158
Trotsky, 125
Turetskii, 155
Turnover tax, 133

Underdeveloped world and growth, 58, 161
Unemployment, equilibrium and, 54
under perfect competition, 45–46
United States, 142, 160
Utility, marginal, 9, 11, 28–33, 47, 48, 50–52, 63, 73, 102
marginal private versus social, 64, 65

Utility *(cont.)*
principle of diminishing marginal, 9, 21–25, 38
total, 9, 28–33

Vaag, 156

Wages, 86, 130, 131
Walras, L., 45, 67
Wants, 1
War Communism, 124
Welfare, economic, 2, 52, 53
noneconomic, 162–164
Welfare economics, 2
Wholesale prices, 132